SEASICK STEVE

MATTHEW WRIGHT

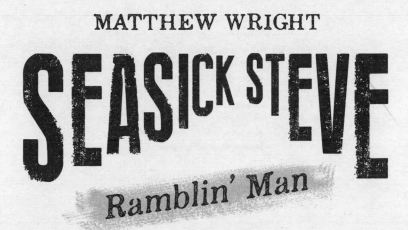

SEASICK STEVE

Ramblin' Man

MUSIC
PRESS

Published by Music Press Books
an imprint of John Blake Publishing Ltd
3 Bramber Court, 2 Bramber Road,
London W14 9PB, England

www.johnblakebooks.com

www.facebook.com/johnblakebooks
twitter.com/jblakebooks

First published in paperback in 2016

ISBN: 978 1 78418 988 4

British Library Cataloguing-in-Publication Data:

A catalogue record for this book is available from the British Library.

Design by www.envydesign.co.uk

Printed in Great Britain by CPI Group (UK) Ltd

5 7 9 10 8 6

Papers used by John Blake Publishing are natural, recyclable products made
from wood grown in sustainable forests. The manufacturing processes conform
to the environmental regulations of the country of origin.

Every attempt has been made to contact the relevant copyright-holders,
but some were unobtainable. We would be grateful if the appropriate people
could contact us.

Contents

CHAPTER 1

31 December 2006: Breakthrough!

It remains one of the most remarkable breakthroughs in music history. Until New Year's Eve 2006, self-styled hobo-blues musician Steven Gene Wold, playing a beat-up, three-string guitar (a.k.a. the 'Three-String Trance Wonder', or 'the biggest piece of shit in the world') and stomping on a wooden box with a Mississippi motorcycle plate stuck on it (the 'Mississippi Drum Machine'), was known only to a tiny community of blues fans. He'd recorded his second album, *Dog House Music*, on an ancient four-track recorder in his kitchen at home in the provincial Norwegian town of Notodden, with only two of his sons for occasional accompaniment.

When he appeared on Jools Holland's *Annual Hootenanny* show that New Year's Eve, Seasick Steve had but two solo albums and a cult fanbase to his name. He was fortunate in having the support of Resonance FM DJ and alternative blues expert Joe Cushley, who had played a crucial role both in encouraging Steve to release the album at all, and then disseminating it among the right musical channels. That said, it doesn't sound as though either Steve or Joe Cushley had any idea what Joe's best efforts would achieve.

It's still hard to take it all in. Steve's vintage recording studio had been reasonably successful on the grunge scene in Olympia, near Seattle, in the 1990s, but had not proved a success when he took it with him to Notodden. He had recorded *Cheap* with the Level Devils in 2002, and released it on his own label in 2004. Meanwhile, he was recuperating from a heart attack. In the two years leading up to his breakthrough, he had begun to build up a small following (including the music journalists Charlie Gillett and Mark Ellen) with a series of gigs at the 12 Bar Club in Denmark Street, Soho. Perhaps he could make a modest, late career as a niche performer? For someone of his age, to all intents and purposes washed up – professionally speaking, anyway – to appear at all on Jools Holland's show was incredible. For him to have so much success, so quickly, and for it to last so long, breaks records left, right and centre.

He's explained the story in detail only a couple of times. If you like hearing Steve's voice – he is a good storyteller – the fullest video account comes in an interview (available on YouTube) that he gave to Rebecca Villiger of Swiss channel SRF 3 in July 2014, recorded while he was in Bern, performing at the Gurtenfestival. It reads at first like a particularly long-winded joke involving three stereotypes walking into a bar, but the ending is much better.

I had a heart attack, I was real sick, and nobody was asking me to play anywhere, not even at the bar down the street. Because of that, I ended up making this record for my wife, not for people, recorded in my kitchen with a tape recorder and two mics. This friend of mine in England [Joe Cushley] called me up to see how I was doing from being sick.

He goes, 'What are you doing, Steve?' And I go, 'Well, I'm in my kitchen, making some songs for my wife.' He goes, 'I really want to hear it.' I go, 'No, man, this is nothing. Matter of fact, it's bad.' And he goes, 'Oh, send it to me, send it to me!' So I sent it to him, and he goes, 'Oh, this is wonderful!' And he gave it somebody else, who used to drive bands around. And one day, this band driver took a band to the Jools Holland show, which is a big show in England. And he saw who the producer was, he had the CD in his back pocket, and he go over and give it to the producer. The guy listened to it, and goes, 'We need to have him on our show.'

There's a little more information in the account Steve gave to Thomas H Green of *The Arts Desk* in June 2011, which contains the names that matter. It's still an astonishing concatenation of good fortune and coincidence, which reads more like the synopsis of a madcap farce than the plans for the release of a record-breaking album.

He [Joe Cushley] asked a few people but no one was interested but this guy Andy [Zammit, the band driver mentioned above], he had a little record company [Bronzerat] putting out records by his girlfriend [Gemma Ray]. Joe told me he'd love to put my record out. I wasn't so interested any more but I called Andy and said, 'I don't care what you do but have you got any money to put it out?' He didn't, so I said, 'How are you going to put it out then?' He borrowed £1,000 from his sister and printed up 900 CDs. Now both Mark Ellen [editor of the now-defunct *Word* magazine] and Charlie Gillett [radio presenter] told [*Later . . . with Jools Holland* producer] Mark Cooper about me – I didn't know about any of this at the time. Andy was driving bands around and he took [American singer-songwriter] Richard Swift to the Jools Holland show and Richard Swift mentioned me to Mark Cooper one more time so they said, 'Yeah, we'd like to see him play.'

On the night, Steve looked uncomfortable as he started singing 'Dog House Boogie', the title track of his latest album, squinting into what he later said was a blinding stage light. But the audience went wild. It was Steve's first appearance as a soloist on any stage remotely this big. He shared the bill that night with much more glitzy and experienced musicians, including Lily Allen and Amy Winehouse, but his novelty and charisma stole the show.

That performance of 'Dog House Boogie' before the dumbstruck *Hootenanny* audience projected Seasick Steve from kitchen performer into the big league. *Dog House Music* sold out overnight. Steve's website – which he claims had a total of about seventy-five hits before the broadcast, sixty of them from himself – crashed, with over a hundred thousand hits by the following morning, and 1,750,000 within the week. The year 2007 brought success beyond his wildest dreams: a MOJO Award for Best Breakthrough Act, and festival appearances at Reading, Leeds and Glastonbury; more gigs, it's said, than any other major artist that year.

The festivals built up. In 2008, his major label debut arrived: *I Started Out With Nothin and I Still Got Most of It Left*, released on Warner Bros. The following year, there was a Brit Award nomination (International Solo Male Artist) and a BBC Four documentary entitled (slightly misleadingly, as it turns out) *Seasick Steve: Bringing It All Back Home*, in which Steve visits places in Mississippi. The rest, as they say, is history.

For both professional reviewers and regular fans, it's Steve's perceived authenticity and raw emotional truth that earned *Dog House Music* such instant acclaim. He's such a captivating storyteller that his listeners assume the events all happened to him exactly as described – and that, in a way, has become a problem. James McNair, writing mainly about Steve's 2013 release *Hubcap Music* in *The Independent* in April 2013, noted, 'One could argue that a key component of Wold's magnetism is that much-coveted commodity, authenticity. The candid, sometimes picaresque lyrics of his autobiographical songs seem hard-won . . .'

Jon Lusk, reviewing for the BBC website, comments on Steve's 'authentic southern atmosphere' and declares that

SEASICK STEVE

'this guy's the real thing'. (Not many other professional
reviews exist of *Dog House Music*: it seems most publications
wanted to wait for the success of Steve's festival
appearances to ensure it was worth their while. It's after
that that the glowing double-page features begin.) But in
both cases Steve's superlative performance leads listeners
to a misleading assumption.

The customer reviews on Amazon, where the album
has a rating of 4.7 out of 5, confirm that it is this quality
that has created such a loyal and adoring fanbase. Again
and again, it's the sense of truth and authenticity, both to
the traditions of the blues and Steve's own raw emotional
state, that listeners perceive in his music. 'Seasick Steve
has lived the blues in the old tradition. His blues is raw
and he is the real deal,' says one. 'His Mississippi roots
shine through each and every song,' says another. 'If
you're a true fan of Delta blues you will love this album.
It's raw, refreshing, and as authentic as Mississippi
mud.' The adulation is almost – dare one say it? – quasi-
religious. 'His live gigs are joyously fervent affairs akin
to a revivalist prayer meeting, but without all the god-
nonsense,' says another fan.

The purist blues has become in many respects a very
hidebound genre, and what many people respond to in
Steve is not so much adherence to the current rules, but his
ability to say something direct, raw and true, in language
that recognisably derives from blues tradition, but does
away with some of its fussier obsessions. The critic Rick
Webb explained it very well, reviewing *Dog House Music*
for the website bluesinlondon.com: 'Steve plays as "real",

"authentic" and "genuine" as anybody around and yet he chooses to do it not in the beard stroking, reverential world of the blues establishment, but in the real world where the only distinction is between "good" and "bad" music.'

Steve has perhaps been the victim of his own success, in that his ability to persuade an audience that he's speaking plainly from the heart applies not just to his performance as a musical actor. It convinces his listeners that he's literally telling the truth about his own life. Even the professional critics believe this: of Steve's stories, the BBC's Jon Lusk says, 'They have the unmistakable ring of truth about them.'

The album's technical deficiencies, its poor acoustics and unvarnished production, as well as the rambling nature of the stories, play directly to the sense that Steve is an artist uninterested in the conventional, time-serving niceties of the modern music business. For many listeners, that makes him more trustworthy.

In addition, for the largely British *Hootenanny* audience (though less so for US audiences, who are usually more critical), his American characteristics play on our susceptibility for straight-talking Southern charmers, and the slide-guitar and dog stories make the whole routine all the more irresistible. Just as Hugh Grant crystallises British stereotypes that a British audience often finds irritating but American audiences love, Steve seems to work in the opposite way, his public persona serving as an encapsulation of everything UK audiences love about the blues, and the Southern United States more generally. As Alex Petridis explained it, reviewing *I Started Out with Nothin . . .* for *The Guardian* in September 2008: 'His story chimes with a certain kind of British music fan's romantic, Cormac McCarthyesque notion of a mythic lost America.'

The romanticism of the hobo life has also helped secure Steve's place in his audience's heart. It's something that works best at a distance, and with a charming accent. Being homeless is a dirty, smelly, depressing business if you see it close up. Few people like it in their own town. A wino with a harmonica and an old dog in the bus station in Birmingham in the UK's West Midlands is usually considered a nuisance; give them a charming accent, dress them in faded check and dungarees, and put them in the sunshine outside the railroad at Birmingham, Alabama, and suddenly they become delightful. The 'hobo' is an American concept, although Steve has famously commented (adapting a definition originally by H L Mencken), on the difference between the hobo, the tramp and the bum, in the UK, that 'tramp' usually has to cover all three. So, if you call yourself a hobo, you're already exotic. We will look in a little more detail at the history of the hobo in due course. It's an important part of Steve's story, and largely unfamiliar to British readers.

Finally, Steve had the advantage of being completely unknown, at least to British viewers, in his current identity. You could surely count on the fingers of one hand the numbers of *Hootenanny* viewers who had previously known about him. Steve was working on a virgin audience, people who'd never read a snarky social media post about him, or a provocative, attention-seeking critical review. There were no preconceived opinions. Steve could, and did, establish an emotive grip on his audience – and New Year's Eve is a good time for emotive grips, with many critical faculties drowned in good cheer, and romance in the air.

There are, then, many reasons – musical, cultural and some specific to the circumstances of Steve's performance – that made it possible for him to establish such a deep and immediate hold on the public's imagination. And those few months either side of the *Hootenanny* appearance were to be the most important years of Steve's musical life to date – though he's had some pretty exciting years since – because that was when his performing career suddenly became viable. That was when it became certain that his music would last.

Now we have to consider what really happened. Sit tight, ladies and gentlemen.

CHAPTER 2

A Story of Several Steves

It might seem unusual to sum up so early on in this book what this writer's research into Steve's life has revealed. But it's necessary, because it changes fundamentally how we regard his biography and musical development. The way Steve presented himself to the world – in terms of appearance, character, age and musical profile – changed, in some ways markedly, in about 2002, when he created Seasick Steve as an artistic identity. The chapters on his early life will make little sense unless that change is explained now.

It's the kind of luck that musical geniuses have, but Steve has just happened upon a whole series of the most exciting episodes in the musical history of twentieth-century popular music, and researching Steve's life has been a fascinating journey, hopping from revolution to revival. His musical background does include several of the most

SEASICK STEVE

exciting episodes from the history of popular music in the past fifty years.

It seemed at the outset as if writing his life would consist of fleshing out many highly entertaining (and a few sad) stories, which all took place in some of the world's most musically evocative locations. Haight-Ashbury? Paris? Clarksdale, Mississippi? Wow! It didn't take long, though, for some of the most basic biographical details presented to the public to unravel in a perplexing way, and this has led to some discoveries that the fans of Steve's stories will find surprising.

Steve's story is a mixture of sporadic, jaw-dropping discoveries and some relatively long periods that have had to be pieced together from scraps of old interview. Contributions from one of his sons, Sevrin Johnson, have filled in some of the gaps, but there are still relatively long periods in the 1970s and 1980s when, although we know approximately where he was and what he was doing, the details are sketchy at best.

We know his birth name is Steve Wold, right? Wrong. Among the many facts about him that have been obscured by the 'Seasick' persona is his name. 'Wold' is his second wife's surname. His original surname is 'Leach', which he used professionally – on his first recording credit, in fact – and continued to use even after he married Norwegian Elisabeth Wold in 1982. It wasn't until the 1990s, when he was living in Olympia, Washington, DC, that he became known to everyone as Steve Wold. In fact, his birth parents probably weren't even called Leach. I have, therefore, settled for just 'Steve' throughout. You know who I mean.

A STORY OF SEVERAL STEVES

Stranger still, someone close to Steve has made a deliberate attempt to create confusion about his age. The ambiguity becomes obvious even from that most familiar of online sources: *Wikipedia*. The English-language page devoted to Steve lists his birth year as 1940/1941, giving his age at time of writing as seventy-four or seventy-five, and this information has been replicated throughout the coverage of his breakthrough and subsequent career. However, go to the Norwegian *Wikipedia* page, and suddenly he's born on 19 March 1951. (Google Translate opens up some fascinating and vital Norwegian resources for those English-speaking fans interested in tracing Steve's career.)

Sevrin Johnson confirmed 1951 as the date of his father's birth too. Moreover, in a fascinating interview that Steve Wold – then owner of Moon Studios – gave in late 2000 to Rick Levin of the Seattle magazine *The Stranger* (still available online, and a must-read for any fan), he announces very candidly, 'I'm fifty years old now.' (He wasn't actually fifty until March 2001, but we can let that pass.) He's similarly open about his age and his original surname 'Leach' in several features about him in the Norwegian press that appeared shortly after his arrival in Norway in 2001.

Why, then, does every English-language feature about Steve published since 2007 overstate his age by ten years? His current policy appears to be to create confusion about his age. On 22 January 2009, in a report about his Brit Award nomination, *The Daily Mail* wrote, 'Although he is said to be sixty-eight, he has refused to confirm his exact age since suffering a near-fatal heart attack five years ago.' "That's just a superstition thing," he chuckles. "Something tells me I might live a bit longer if I don't talk about my age."' In fact, he was fifty-seven at the time. And the heart attack doesn't explain why the estimate of his age is still out by ten years.

The same thing happened in July 2014, during an interview with Swiss channel SRF 3 while he was performing at the Gurtenfestival in Bern. The interviewer began her question by stating, 'You are over seventy years old.' Steve shrugged, said, 'That's what they say,' and refrained from giving a precise figure. A press release dating from 2009 and produced by Neuland Concerts – a division of Warner Music Germany – suggests similar obfuscation. It begins by bemoaning the inaccuracy of a large amount of coverage about Steve, then goes on to present 'the facts, so far as he remembers them, are as follows'. It continues, 'Steve Wold was born in Oakland, in the San Francisco Bay Area around the post-war period,' but stops short of providing a more precise a date. It's not the date of 1941 that is still listed on *Wikipedia* and many standard bios, but it's sufficiently vague to create doubt about his chronology. It could be suggested that Steve knew exactly when he was born when he was talking to Seattle's *The Stranger* in 2000.

The explanation emerges when we look more closely at the chronology of his life that he began presenting when he became Seasick Steve in 2003. In 'Dog House Boogie' he writes, 'I left home 'fore I was fourteen years of age; I figured I'd do better on my own / But then followed eleven years of bumblin' around and livin' kinda hand-in-mouth / Sometimes gettin' locked up an' somet– sometimes just goin' cold and hungry / I didn't have me no real school education, so what in the hell what I was gonna be able to do?'

One possible explanation for the sudden change in his birth date is that he decided, soon after writing the song, that to be fully convincing he needed to have spent longer as a hobo than the space available in his actual biography, and the 'eleven years of bumblin' around' are why, as of about 2003 (the date of his full live debut as Seasick Steve, when his hobo mythology began to take hold), he suddenly became ten years older than he really was. His age was an invention that was necessary to create space in his biography for an extensively exaggerated hobo life story. It may be that Steve spent some parts of the mid- and late 1960s living as an itinerant worker, moving from farm to funfair as the seasons and demand dictated, and for some of that time, he was sleeping rough. He does seem to have had some kind of first-hand experience. And it was almost certainly in California, not Mississippi.

Steve's son Sevrin believes that Steve does have genuine experience of living rough from his late teens: 'That part of his life was really only a couple years, I'm guessing between eighteen and twenty-ish . . . it's his gimmick, you know.' 'Gimmick' was Sevrin's choice of words, but, looking at how the biography was presented, it seems pretty accurate.

There are no doubts that Steve's home life was horribly tough, and that he left when he was fourteen, give or take a year or two. If he was born in 1951, that would have made him fourteen in 1965 when he left home in Oakland and moved only a couple of miles over the Bay Bridge to San Francisco. He's always been open about having spent some time in San Francisco's Haight-Ashbury district, between 1965 and 1967. In fact, before he invented Seasick Steve, he claimed to have been there the whole time – and what music-loving teenager would leave somewhere like that to sit alone on a train in Mississippi?

By mid-1969, we know he was in the Bay Area again, and stayed there, working as a musician until shortly before he left for Paris. The years 1967–72 were very likely important musical years, when he played with the Beach Boys, Son House, Janis Joplin, Joni Mitchell and Lightnin' Hopkins. So you would expect that as much of this time as possible was spent playing guitar in San Francisco, rather than wandering around the countryside. He left for France with his first wife, Victoria Johnson, in 1972. After that (apart from some time in 1980–1, after he left Victoria and their two sons, when he was probably busking through Europe) it's clear where he was living after 1972 – and it wasn't on a train in Mississippi.

We can be absolutely sure that Steve was a working musician in or around San Francisco for most of the time between leaving home in 1965 and going to France in 1972. As Steve Leach, he has a credit playing bass on an album released in 1971, with a band that was touring and later recording for substantial chunks of 1970 and 1971. The album's liner notes establish beyond all doubt that the Steve Leach playing bass is our own Seasick Steve.

This was the most astonishing discovery of all, though it's been there in the public domain all along if you know where to look. The band Steve was a member of in 1970–2 – Shanti – was dedicated to promulgating Transcendental

Meditation. Although the TM movement was widespread among musicians, especially Californian ones, in the late sixties, that kind of scenester musical image is totally at odds with the plain-speaking, train-riding image most fans have of Seasick Steve. And, although there is less conclusive evidence to prove it, the likelihood is that Transcendental Meditation remained important to Steve for another twenty years at least. Those are two plausible reasons why his past had to be rewritten.

Shanti was a band formed of players from the Bay Area, and in order to join a band like that, which was well connected, and signed to a major label, Steve would have required a reputation and contacts in the area, so he must have already had substantial experience on the scene. Not only that, but the Transcendental Meditation was the essence of the band's identity – all of the musicians in the band wanted to promote this philosophy. There is a YouTube video of Shanti performing, probably in 1971, when Steve was only twenty. He was wearing a green-and-pink Hawaiian shirt and tight beige trousers, and certainly didn't look as if he'd crawled out of a boxcar. He also didn't look like the incredible guitarist we know today. His hair is already receding, and he has a little beard. In other photos in the album booklet he sports a fine pair of muttonchop whiskers and a handlebar moustache.

One of the conclusive pieces of evidence about Steve's involvement in Shanti is a whole-page feature about the band in *Rolling Stone* on 25 May 1972 by Charles Perry, one of the magazine's most prolific writers, who later penned *The Haight-Ashbury: A History*. Although in terms of rock journalism there could hardly have been a more obvious place to look for Steve's musical background, the British press never seemed to have linked it with Steve – presumably because it uses his surname 'Leach'. It would seem that Steve's real identity is an open secret among parts of the American musical press, one they have tacitly agreed to keep as long as he doesn't perform there too much.

In general terms, Perry's piece confirms in sometimes amusing detail the fact that Steve was a musician, hippie and Transcendental Meditator in the late 1960s, but there is room for doubt about his whereabouts in the middle of that decade. This article contains a hint that he may, perhaps, have been genuinely homeless soon after he left home – which Perry gives as 1964 – when Steve may have been as young as twelve (if he left before 19 March that year). Perry describes the band members' musical genesis at length, including the following passage:

> Neil Seidel [Shanti's lead guitarist] had been playing guitar in the Los Angeles City College jazz band in 1964 while he was still in high school, right around the time Steve Leach... was running away from home in Oakland, at the age of twelve . . .

In 1966, Steve 'was still running from home', Perry adds. This could just mean that Steve was wary, as he often has been, of revealing too much detail about his whereabouts and activities. He has said elsewhere that he was in Haight-Ashbury from 1965 to 1967, at least. But it could also suggest that Steve was genuinely homeless for a period of time straight after *leaving* home, and was too embarrassed to go into details about it.

There are psychological reasons, too, why it also seems likely that he spent the crucial period 1967–72 in California rather than riding trains in the Deep South. He'd fallen on his feet, after a horrific childhood, and just seen arguably the most exciting two years in popular music happen right before his eyes. He'd made some friends, had good company for the first time in his life, not least in the Transcendental Meditation community. This must make it more likely that he should stay, than go, the spaced-out creative community around San Francisco offering, perhaps, some of the familial warmth he'd recently lacked.

We don't know for certain when he met Victoria Johnson, but it was sometime before 1970. In the video of Steve playing bass with Shanti, he appears to be wearing a wedding ring, which would imply a very early marriage. Yet, for someone with a background of such insecurity, that sort of desire for stability would be understandable. Victoria was from California, and offering her the life of a hobo across the far side of the country seems an unlikely way to cement the relationship.

Even in Steve's official version, his hobo life stopped in 1973. As Sean O'Hagan explains, with nuance, in *The Guardian* in 2008, 'Though both his songs and his persona trade heavily on his hobo credentials, he actually turned his back on the road way back in 1973. "It just got too damn hard," he says, "and I knew if I kept on, I'd end up dead in a ditch somewhere." The trajectory of his life since then is hazy and, one suspects, he plays down the semi-settled years, sensing correctly that his mainly young audience prefer the myth to the reality.' O'Hagan is certainly right about the myth, as we saw in the responses to Steve in the previous chapter, but that myth is much more extensive than previously realised.

The 'eleven years of bumblin' around' isn't the only occasion on which an exaggerated image of Steve's hobo lifestyle seems to have been presented. The next part of that lyric – 'I didn't have me no real school education, so what in the hell what I was gonna be able to do?' – was true of this point in Steve's life in the early 1970s, but not later. One of the tensions in his marriage to Victoria that eventually contributed to bringing the marriage down was a constant lack of money, and it's something that he seemed determined to avoid when he married his second wife, Elisabeth. So when they moved back to the USA from Norway, and settled in Tennessee, Steve eventually enrolled himself in college and, as a mature student, got himself a professional qualification.

In fact, he does seem to have left some interesting questions in his wake on his journeys from one place to the next. The recording studios he set up in Olympia and Notodden are well known now, but he also had a studio in Tennessee for a while that didn't work out, which he doesn't talk about. On the other hand, he told Seattle magazine *The Stranger* in 2000 that he'd had a studio in Europe, which seems unlikely. It's as if he's trying to keep the press away from everything that's really happened to him, even if, at times, that means creating a fantasy alternative. Given his family background, and the extreme degree of self-reliance he had to learn at an early age, that's understandable. Close up he's also seen a lot of stars who didn't handle stardom well – including Janis Joplin, Jimi Hendrix and Kurt Cobain – and their experiences may have affected his own attitude to rock fame.

Steve has had a favourable run in the British media, with his entire hobo story repeated with little scrutiny by everyone from broadsheet newspapers and the BBC to the *West Briton*, his local paper in Cornwall, where he eventually settled. In 2009, BBC Four even took him on a jolly trip around Mississippi for the documentary *Seasick Steve: Bring It All Back Home*, though it's far from clear he has ever lived in Mississippi, either as a hobo or as anything else. He did live near Nashville in Tennessee (where, in fairness, some of the BBC Four programme was filmed) for a few years in the 1980s. Tennessee also has a fine country music tradition, but Steve certainly wasn't a hobo then: he was newly married to his second wife, whom he'd go on to have three children with, and alongside his musical work was at college and had a respectable job.

Understandably, he kept his relationships private, but he clearly rates the value of a long-term companionship, and in his adult life has had long-term partnerships with two women. As far as we can tell, he met Victoria in San Francisco when they were both teenagers enjoying the Summer of Love (or possibly soon afterwards). In the 1970s, he travelled first to France with her, and then Hawaii, and in each place they had a son. His travelling stories from any time after 1970 must be balanced against the fact that, apart from a brief period in 1980 when he was between marriages, he always had one or another of his wives, and often several young children, with him at the time.

After that marriage broke up in 1980, and during a busking tour of Europe, Steve met Norwegian waitress Elisabeth Wold while singing in a bar in Oslo. They married in 1982, and from then on he has led a settled, even conventional, family life, first in Tennessee, then Olympia, Washington, DC (with a brief spell in Hawaii in between), then Norway and finally Cornwall. If one is looking for features that connect the places where Steve has lived – rather than anything to do with trains or the Deep South – surfing looks the likely one. Hawaii, the West Coast of the US and Cornwall all have that – if not much else – in common. In recent years, he has seemed to grow weary of the prominence that his hobo stories have attracted, and it's probably no coincidence that his most recent album has focused on surfing, the one pastime that he has undoubtedly engaged in his whole adult life, rather than reheat some tales of life on the road.

For obvious reasons, Steve has not wanted to participate in research for this biography. This has meant that there are several stretches of his life that it is not possible to reconstruct in detail. For example, the time spent in Haight-Ashbury communes, his musical career immediately after that and the years of European busking are not reliably documented. I am grateful to Sevrin, Steve's eldest son, by his first marriage to Victoria Johnson, for filling in the details of some of this time, and for a little more about their bittersweet relationship.

Sadly, other avenues of investigation appear to have been closed off. Steve spent much of the 1980s, just after his second marriage, training and then practising as a professional in Tennessee. Because the college education and responsible, practical, middle-class nature of it conflicts directly with his hobo image, this part of his career has been most assiduously hushed up.

There is an amusing post on Yahoo! Answers – only a couple of years old, and still viewable at the time of writing – by one of Steve's former professional colleagues. It is a response to the question 'Why did "Seasick Steve" take his wifes [sic] name when he married her in 1982?', and was written by a man called Joe, claiming to be one of Steve's colleagues from his time as a paramedic in Tennessee. Joe had only just discovered that the Steve Leach he knew as a family man and fellow professional living in suburban Franklin, Tennessee, was now telling stories of a hobo life that Steve in 1988 knew nothing of, or certainly kept very quiet about. So I contacted a relevant professional organisation in Tennessee, hoping to find out more about the old Steve. After a friendly initial greeting, and a promise to get back to me as soon as they had information, there was nothing. No 'Sorry, no one knows anything.' Just silence. Rightly or wrongly, one cannot help feel that Steve had been in touch to suggest that this kind of comment is not helpful. And people wonder why he goes by the name of Seasick Steve and never tours the USA. Among Californian musicians, several of whom Steve performed with in the 1960s and 1970s, his dual identity as Steve Leach/Wold appears to be an open secret, and, if he performed there more often than he does, it would surely have been spoken of by now.

Likewise, his years in Olympia have been harder to trace than expected because of a similar outbreak of collective amnesia. He became something of a fixture on the musical scene in a crucial period of exciting music-making (Steve has a habit, throughout his life, of turning up at those). Although clearly not as famous as Olympia's superstar, Kurt Cobain, or even the most successful band he worked with, Modest Mouse, or the founder of K Records, Calvin Johnson, Steve did run a guitar shop, then a studio, for nearly a decade, and certainly had a local presence. One interview from that period refers to him as 'producer and Northwest icon Steve Wold'. Anyone actively involved in the local scene would have known who he was. Yet despite a request from the respected local radio station, KAOS, no one seemed able to remember anything.

Fortunately, in the later 1990s the Internet began to take the place of fragile human memories, and both from Olympia, and especially from the time Steve moved to Norway in 2001, it's possible to follow most of his work online. Readers who want to trace Steve's transformation for themselves can still find a treasure trove of coverage on the website of Norwegian local newspaper *Telen*, which covers the Notodden area, where Steve once lived. You can see his fascinating transformation from west-coast hippie with a haystack beard, straight out of the grunge scene in Olympia, into his hobo outfit of dungarees and check shirt. Intriguingly, the Neuland Concerts press release presenting his 2009 album *Man From Another Time*

24

states, inaccurately, that Steve and his family lived in Oslo – as do some newspaper features from around that time. Such an obvious error could be taken as an attempt to put readers off the *Telen* scent, because the *Telen* reports paint a clear, and very different picture of Seasick Steve's evolution.

Somewhere in the middle are the first performances of Seasick Steve and the Level Devils, with Steve wearing a white T-shirt and new indigo jeans, his bald dome glistening in the stage lights (see, for example, the review by Knut H Slettemo, published on 26 April 2003). There's no John Deere cap at this point, and the guitar looks in good condition, with all the strings present and correct. It's a completely different look – not without a touch of the dad-rocker, if we're honest – from the authentic-looking hobo who appeared on Jools Holland's *Hootenanny*.

The important thing for lovers of Steve's music – which is what this should all be about, after all – is that it's difficult to think of anyone who has dedicated more of their life to music. Pretty much everything we know about Steve tells us that, family aside (or included, in the case of his first marriage), his entire life has been dedicated to playing and recording great songs. Childhood, teenage years, everything he did as an adult, apart from some of his professional life in Tennessee (and even that was playing the long game towards the foundation of Moon Studios) was focused on his love of the art form.

For fans who are disappointed to discover that some of the details in the Seasick Steve story have been presented with a particular emphasis in order to bring it to life, there are extenuating circumstances. He created the identity when he was completely unknown, and his fame – when it came – came almost overnight, with no opportunity to plan how he would respond to public attention. He can have had no idea where he would end up. His hobo alter ego and musical affair with the Deep South seem to have begun in a dispute with some Norwegian musicians, who were sceptical about his American musical roots.

His retreat into the old blues world of Mississippi, which doesn't seem to have featured in his life even when he was on the road, was most likely a defiant act of the imagination, forging a musical and cultural identity he could call his own, against a Norwegian music scene he didn't really fit into – and which didn't, in some respects, give him the respect he wanted. In something of a standoff with parts of the Norwegian music scene, which was appropriating a musical culture Steve felt, with some justice, he knew best, he seems to be trying to show that he was the more authentic bluesman.

He reached deep inside himself in a crucial and desperate moment in his career, and created something that drew on his early experiences with bluesmen such as K C Douglas and Lightnin' Hopkins, but also on the eclecticism of the Grateful Dead, the dark humour of Modest Mouse, the angry edges of some the spikier bands he helped produce, such as Murder City Devils. By the time he came to write that misleading lyric on 'Dog House Boogie', he didn't even have the Level Devils, but was writing the album at home. He can't have had the faintest idea it would be dissected for biographical accuracy ten years later. The hobo genie escaped the bottle in a way he could never have expected.

What's even odder is that the life he really led – mainly playing music and working with some great musicians – is a much more fertile one artistically than it would have been if he'd spent it riding trains on his own. The great blues musicians had mostly left Mississippi (or died) by the time Steve is supposed to have been there. There were many more of them in California, where Steve actually spent the 1960s. That was where he learned the blues, and other kinds of music his fans have no idea he could play.

Even during the period after he claimed his hobo life ended, in 1972 or 1973, he hasn't acknowledged that he played with some stellar musicians, including blues guitarist Albert King and Slash from Guns N' Roses. The more recent evidence is harder to piece together than what he did in 1965–72 (for which some surprising evidence has emerged), but there is reliable testimony from a wide range of people, including many pre-'Seasick' comments from Steve himself, to suggest that, essentially, his whole life has been in music. Although all three of Steve's sons with Elisabeth have been involved to some degree in his musical career, in general he has been keen to protect his marriage and family – two things that rarely come out of rock stardom well – from press interest.

To judge from his comments and demeanour in interviews, a rather sad change has come over a musician previously so proud of his involvement with an impressive and diverse array of stars. Online, there is an obscure but hugely revealing interview with the Tremens – one of

Steve's favourite bands from his studio in Olympia; it is undated, but probably from 2001, when their second and last album was released. The band members, greatly in awe of Steve's experience, reveal a musician with an exciting, inspiring performing past. Quentin Ertel, the guitarist, says, 'One of the big things Steve has done for us and this band is simply to be able to know and interact with someone with his kind of history and his kind of accomplishments under his belt. I'm not just talking about the records he's recorded here in the [Pacific] Northwest that have gone on to be really influential, I'm also talking about the bands that he's played with over the years.'

The first difference that is apparent between the man Ertel knew and the Seasick Steve of today is that in his earlier incarnation Steve was obviously proud of his musical past, and keen to share his stories. As we look over his recent, post-*Hootenanny* responses to questions about his musical experience, and the non-musical work he's done alongside it, there's no doubt that a veil of silence has fallen over his pre-2003 musical career. Both in Olympia and on arrival in Norway, he was expansive, repeatedly telling the local newspaper *Telen* about the range of exciting musicians he used to hang out with. This paragraph, from an article published in the newspaper in April 2003, previewing his premiere as Seasick Steve in Notodden, Norway, is typical:

> Steve turned increasingly back to around [sic] San Francisco, and the last half of the Sixties, he played with legends like Lightnin' Hopkins, Chuck Berry,

John Lee Hooker and Freddie King, he warmed up for Son House, traded guitar riffs with Mike Bloomfield and Jerry Garcia, knew Janis Joplin and was at the right place at the right time. Since he began a life as a professional musician, he has worked among others with artists like [sic] The Beach Boys, Joni Mitchell and Kenny Rogers.

After he became 'Seasick', those stories went quiet.

The second change is in his attitude to fame, which John Mitchell expresses so memorably. Steve has actually been rubbing shoulders with famous musicians since the age of fifteen, on and off. He had probably met all of the members of rock's infamous '27 Club' – and seems to have known a couple of them well, as we'll see in due course. So he has observed close-up the damage fame can do, and, although it's obvious from his personal history that he always wanted to make a living from music, he does seem to have enjoyed being in the background, not being the guy in the spotlight. The situation he had with Modest Mouse – he went on tour with them occasionally, played guitar on some recordings, and has even appeared in their video of *Dashboard* (2007) as a bartender with a false leg made from a guitar neck – seems to have suited him just about right. Now, of course, he has no choice about the limelight, as long as he continues to perform – but one might argue that 'Seasick Steve' is a protective mask to keep public interest at a safe distance from someone who's never really wanted to be famous.

There were two stages to the creation of Seasick Steve as

we know him today. The first, which took place in Norway in 2003–6, was his creation of the name, character and his trademark early songs. In many ways, this was a reaction against the failure of his studio and the dissatisfaction he felt at his reception in Notodden. At the time, he was performing to a few hundred people at most, and can never have imagined that the lyrics he wrote for the songs on *Cheap* and *Back in the Doghouse* would be taken as autobiographical fact by millions. The second stage, when he suddenly became famous, was to refrain from commenting on his previous life, and insist that everything on his first two albums was completely true.

Although most of Steve's fans clearly adore his 'Seasick' persona, once you've spent time looking at his history, it's pretty clear that the truth about Steve is much more interesting than the rather fantastical past he's created for himself. It's also much more *possible*, musically. In some interviews he has presented himself as a kind of evening hobby player, who strums a few chords after a day at his blue-collar job. But it is unlikely that a guitarist of his skill could have emerged onto the scene as he has done without significant professional playing experience beforehand.

Which is why, all told, it's very sad that Steve won't talk publicly about the amazing musicians he's worked with over the years. In the nicest possible way, there's a touch of Jekyll and Hyde about Steve Leach/Wold and Seasick Steve. In the search for the ultimate musical expression of his idiosyncratic bruised and battered persona, he's brilliantly recreated the country blues with invigorating punk flavours.

In 2007, the hobo connotations that surround Steve attracted great interest, but latterly he has appeared to grow tired of the importance placed on it by interviewers, preferring instead to emphasise the mundane jobs he did to bring up his kids. In an interview with the website unshredded.net on 14 October 2010, in response to the standard hobo question, he replied,

> Yeah, I mean, because that happened a long time ago, and it all got a bit strange people thinking that I just crawled out from under a rock a year ago, but I've raised five children, my boy is thirty-five years old, I didn't do that living on trains, I had lots of normal jobs, whacking a hammer, doing plumbing, I sold shoes, I did anything man, so most of my adult life, I've had a lot of jobs. Job after job after job after job.

He still doesn't refer to his professional career here, but it's a significant shift of emphasis. The same sentiments were repeated as recently as July 2014, in his interview with Swiss channel SRF 3. When the interviewer ran through a summary of his hobo and busking career, Steve replied, 'Yeah, I did that stuff you're talking about when I was young. I have five boys, and most of the time I was trying to raise my children, and I didn't really play music much.' In the course of this book, we will turn to other accounts that suggest he did play a bit more than that, and that it did conflict with home life.

It's notable, too, that later albums have had much less to

say about trains and the hobo lifestyle. It's a gradual shift: *I Started Out With Nothin And I Still Got Most Of It Left* includes 'The Log Cabin', a classic rambling tale about being unable to settle in one place, which implies a travelling life, but less explicitly so than the tales on Steve's first two albums.

Man From Another Time contains the song 'Just Because I Can (CSX)', in which Steve sings, 'Gonna find me a southbound CSX / Gonna ride all day for free.' (CSX Corporation is a Florida-based railroad company.) There's also 'Never Go West', and 'Dark', both seemingly about the life of a hobo, but without the particulars of life on the road that the first albums had in abundance. They are more of a philosophical statement about the travelling condition than a practical travelogue in the style of early songs such as *Cheap*'s 'Hobo Blues'. There are songs about tractors ('Big Green and Yeller') or the feeling of being from another era (the title track), but no details about the rootless existence of a poor traveller.

By the time we reach *You Can't Teach An Old Dog New Tricks* (2011), the lyrics have become even generalised. Some of the same themes emerge that were present on earlier albums (on 'Back in the Doghouse', for example), but, aside from hints in songs such as 'Whiskey Ballad', all references to trains and life on the road is gone. *Hubcap Music* (2013) continues this allusive approach. 'Self Sufficient Man' might be about the independence of the hobo way of life, but the details are vague. The lines 'I been wanderin' the world around / I seen and done more things / Than you could imagine / In your wildest dreams' could imply a reference to that itinerant lifestyle, but could equally well apply to many others too. The same goes for 'Freedom Road': it's general enough to be about any number of things. There's another nod to rustic living with 'Down on the Farm' and 'Home', but overall the album is less tied to vignettes of hobo existence than Steve's earlier efforts.

In fact, farming and cars – which don't turn up much in the first few albums – have become an increasingly prominent theme in Steve's work. On the one hand, cars were in his family, and his first guitar lesson was with bluesman K C Douglas, whose best-known song is about a car. It seems to give him a good reason to hang out in dungarees and check, sound rustic and appeal to the right demographic without being tied to hobo life.

Videos for songs such as 'Down on the Farm' have proved popular too, with the *Top Gear* end of his fans (he appeared on the TV show in 2010). In April 2013, during an interview with *The Independent* for the release of *Hubcap Music*, he revealed, 'I would like to take some time off to do some farming. It's an amazing feeling to plough, to plant something and see it come up.' In a piece in *The Sun* from April 2015, Steve describes his *Top Gear* appearance as 'the funniest time I ever had . . . almost', and expresses his regret about the sacking of presenter Jeremy Clarkson. It does seems a bit unlikely than ten minutes on Clarkson's sofa really cuts it for a musician who's hung out with Janis Joplin in Haight-Ashbury, played guitar with John Paul Jones and Jack White, and witnessed more epochal moments in the history of rock and blues than a BBC Four documentary. It's also difficult to imagine Steve the hippie, bemoaning America's addiction to the profit motive in his interview in Seattle's *The Stranger* in 2000, finding much in common politically with Jeremy Clarkson, either.

The lyrics on his latest album, *Sonic Soul Surfer* (2015) – the most successful album since *Man From Another Time* – deal least of all with the hobo life. Many of the songs refer to favourite old themes – 'Dog Gonna Play' or 'We Be Moving' – but are largely stripped of specific narrative or lifestyle references.

We have to bear certain factors in mind before assessing the ways in which Steve has spoken about his biography. Between the release of the first two Seasick Steve albums, his life had deteriorated in several important ways. He'd moved to a new continent to make a new start, but hadn't settled into the Norwegian musical community. His studio business wasn't going well and then he had a heart attack. In August 2005, he sold his final 31.8 per cent share of the Juke Joint Studio for a tiny fraction of its value.

A dispute with the Norwegian musical community made him reluctant to release *Cheap* on a local label, so he created his own label – There's A Dead Skunk Records. At first, it operated from an address in Clarksdale, Mississippi – apparently to demonstrate the strength of his blues connections to the Notodden blues community in general, and particularly his then-manager Morten Gjerde, who was keen for Steve to release *Cheap* on the local label Bluestown Records, which Gjerde part-owns. (There's A Dead Skunk Records is now officially established as part of Steve's intellectual property, but wasn't initially.) The character of 'Seasick Steve' seems to be an extension of that process, in a way – he was trying to prove he was rooted in the blues tradition. And he succeeded beyond his wildest dreams.

Given his heart attack, he may only have been half joking when he said he created *Dog House Music* to give his wife something to listen to after he was gone. Psychologically, then, those feelings of rejection, depression and isolation were very real. He was rootless and seems to have had nowhere he felt at home.

Several journalists have picked up on the large number of homes that Steve has had over the years. Sean O'Hagan explained it succinctly in *The Guardian* in September 2008: 'Though he has been married to his second wife for twenty-seven years, and has five grown-up sons, Steve has had some trouble putting down roots in one place. "I'm a settled hobo" is how he puts it, adding that he and his wife have lived in fifty-nine different houses to date.' And it's true that even when everything else was going well for him – his second marriage and kids seem to have been a great source of joy – he was still restless, and has made regular, long-distance moves. Even if the image of his hobo life has been exaggerated, there was certainly something hobo-like about his state of mind.

There's no doubt that Steve has made a substantial contribution to the subgenre of hobo music. The history and culture of the hobo in the USA is alien for British readers, and it's such an important part of Steve's story that it's worth familiarising ourselves with its history. For British fans, 'tramp' – our only equivalent – doesn't come close. The concept sometimes seems exotic, romantic, even glamorous (a cultural resonance Steve has unintentionally exploited), but was historically, for the most part, associated with the most miserable, grinding poverty.

Steve's own definition of a hobo is fairly well known. He shared it with Michael Hubbard of *musicOMH* in August 2008:

> 'I'll tell ya,' he rumbles, looking for all the world like a kindly garage mechanic with his long grey beard and baseball cap. 'There are three different names. One's a hobo, one's a tramp and one's a bum. You was a hobo, and people used to be very particular if they fell in that category, if you rode the freight trains looking for work. You was a tramp, you rode the freight trains and tried not to work. If you was a bum you didn't ride trains, you didn't even go nowhere and you didn't work. Those are the three names before you got the word "homeless"'. He sips his coffee and looks wistful. 'And that was a long time ago.'

In fact, this is only a colloquial version of the definition that US writer H L Mencken gave in his book *The American Language* (1937). The distinctions between the three kinds of homeless were widely known in the USA, and carried some significance. That may well be because within living memory, there were many Americans who were at least temporarily homeless, and they guarded the dignity of their status jealously. In a culture where social and material success is so crucial, even the distinctions between the homeless and unemployed matter. That said, attitudes to hobos in popular music have generally been negative.

The history of the hobo goes back as far as there have been trains – before the first appearance of the word, in fact. It's believed that discharged soldiers first jumped trains to return home after the Civil War in the 1860s. The largest single cause of hobo travel was, of course, the Great Depression in 1930s, though the Great Migration of poor black workers from the Deep South to the industrial cities of the North, which continued sporadically for much of the last century until about 1970, also created many hobo travellers, at least temporarily.

The term 'hobo' appeared some time after the type of person it would define, first being recorded in the 1890s in California. The origin of the word is uncertain. The most common theory is that it derives from 'hoe-boy', a term used to distinguish hobos working the land from the general worker, just a 'boy'. The town of Hoboken in New Jersey has also been linked to the term; in the nineteenth century, it was a terminus for many railway lines. But no one really knows for sure.

There is a hobo sign language used by the community to indicate which places are safe and which aren't, where food, water, shelter, medical care and work may be found, and where danger (dogs or zealous police, for example) exists. Thus, two circles linked together denotes handcuffs, meaning that hobos are jailed here; two shovels indicate that manual work is available. There are reports of instances when opportunistic journalists have ambushed Steve to test him on these emblems without warning. He's always passed the test. The basics of these signs are simple and easy to pick up, however, so this doesn't prove that Steve has spent more than a short while on the road.

In terms of his life story, by far the most important piece of hobo history connected with Steve is the tradition of the hobo song, which has existed for as long as the hobo himself. There is now quite a collection of songs about hobo life, mostly dating from the middle of the last century, when memories were still fresh of large numbers of itinerants travelling to find work during the Great Depression of the 1930s. One of the reasons, perhaps, that audiences are quick to assume that Steve is singing directly about his own life is that British audiences, at least, are not familiar with this tradition. Very few other singers of hobo songs have been hobos themselves. It's a surprisingly popular topic, lending itself equally to blues, folk and country singers, and – albeit in a more sarcastic vein – to some mainstream comic pop singers as well.

The singers who chose this subject often display very different attitudes towards this unfortunate character. Some are sympathetic, some contemptuous, some make a joke of him; but most of these hobo songs present a clear sense that being a hobo is a shameful thing. There is one big innovation in this tradition, however, that Seasick Steve was the first to attempt – quite brilliantly – as we shall see.

Folk singer Goebel Reeves wrote one of the most famous hobo songs in the 1930s, 'Hobo's Lullaby' – perhaps the most sympathetic of all such songs. It was performed by many of America's most luminous folk and country singers, including Woody Guthrie, Pete Seeger, Emmylou Harris and bluesman Ramblin' Jack Elliott, whom Steve knew a little. It runs, 'Do not think 'bout tomorrow / Let tomorrow come and go / Tonight you're in a nice warm boxcar / Safe from all that wind and snow.' In this account being a hobo is pitiable; indeed, even when the singer takes a generally kindly attitude towards the hobo, there's almost always a hint of the shame and distaste with which they were usually regarded.

Jimmie Rodgers's famous 'Hobo Bill's Last Ride' (1929) is also broadly sympathetic, though there's a sense in this tale – concerning the death of the eponymous character on an overnight train – of emotional distance from the protagonist, who is half colourful wanderer, half irresponsible alien. The last verse presents a character whose happy-go-lucky lifestyle turns into something a little tragic and despicable:

> *It was early in the morning when they raised the hobo's head*
> *The smile still lingered on his face but Hobo Bill was dead*
> *There was no mother's longing to soothe his weary soul*
> *For he was just a railroad bum who died out in the cold.*

There's a similar mixture of pity and contempt in 'The Hobo Song'. This song is best known as part of the bluegrass band Old and in the Way's self-titled 1975 album (featuring Jerry Garcia on banjo). It was composed and released in 1972 by San Francisco session musician Jack Bonus, who sings in a more emotive, soulful way that's overall better suited to the lyric. Although less familiar than many of the others songs in the genre, it's one of the most poignant, concerning an 'old hobo lost out in the rain', who left 'a wife and five children who live in LA . . . Oh, they miss their dear daddy who's gone so far away.' The hobo 'used to be a gambling man / Just like you / Until he sank so low / That there was nothin' that no one could do.' Despite the fact that the sympathy here is clearly genuine, there's still an implication that this man has gone to the bad and deserves his fate.

Bonus was, intriguingly, active in the Bay Area in the late sixties, and has established connections to some of the Bay's biggest bands. His album was released on Grunt Records, established by Jefferson Airplane to take on less commercial projects. The Airplane themselves apparently later covered 'Sweet Mahidabelle' from the album, and Bonus's contacts with both the Airplane and Jerry Garcia suggest he was a familiar figure from the scene, who may well – though we can't be sure – have known Steve at some point.

Roger Miller's 'King of the Road' (covered by a range artists, including Elvis Presley) is at least cheerful, although the tone veers between celebrating the hobo's freedom and mocking his limited resources. And Paul Simon's 'Papa Hobo' offers a wistful vignette that's certainly not unkind, but still presents the hobo as a remote and unfortunate figure.

Not everyone was so generous. 'Hobo' Jack Turner, a comic creation of singer Ernie Hare, who was active in the 1920s and 1930s, presents a light-hearted but also rather callous and complacent view of a hobo's life as one of carefree drifting. The song 'I'm Glad I'm a Bum' (1930) begins, 'I'm glad I'm a bum, a bummy bum bum / I'm ragged but happy, I'm glad I'm a bum . . .' 'The Bum Song', from the previous year, is, if anything, worse, presenting the homeless traveller as something of a freeloader, living in a 'nest' and on the scrounge. (This could be because it's about a bum rather than a real hobo, though that's not a distinction 'Hobo' Jack Turner seems to have been very interested in making.) Curiously, 'The Bum Song' contains passages of spoken narration not unlike some of Seasick Steve's stories, though it seems unlikely Steve would have used 'Hobo' Jack as a model.

Other humorous takes on the character include Louis Armstrong's kindlier 'Hobo, You Can't Ride This Train' (1932), while Harry McClintock's 'Big Rock Candy Mountain' (1928), perhaps the best known of all these hobo songs, offers a comically caring vision of hobo utopia, though the reality (bulldogs don't have rubber teeth and alcohol doesn't trickle down the rocks) is never far from the listener's mind – that's McClintock's joke, of course. For a Canadian perspective, there's Wilf Carter's similarly genial 'Hobos' Song of the Mounties' (1934).

In some ways, the most surprising of these songs is Bob Dylan's 'Only a Hobo' (1963), which, unexpectedly – given Dylan's reputation as a revolutionary social thinker – continues the implication of the title in dismissing the hobo as an individual without dignity. These lines in particular have a sour ambivalence. Yes, Dylan is asking, in a half-sympathetic way, what it takes out of a man to see his life slide down the pan as a hobo. But there's no disguising the bewilderment – verging on disgust – that Dylan feels towards someone who's let that happen:

Does it take much of a man to see his whole life go down
To look up on the world from a hole in the ground
To wait for your future like a horse that's gone lame
To lie in the gutter and die with no name?

Steve's clearest musical hobo ancestor, both in terms of musical style and treatment of the character, is John Lee Hooker, who recorded a well-known song entitled 'Hobo Blues', released as a single in 1948. It was also covered by R L Burnside, with whom (according to a March 2006 piece on bluesinlondon.com) Steve played in Seattle. Hooker had himself travelled from his home town of Clarksdale in Mississippi to Detroit, via Memphis and Cincinnati, riding trains hobo-style at least part of the way. The song is partly about someone who has to become a hobo. It's clear from Hooker's lyric, however, that the whole process is both shameful and tragic. The opening lines – 'When I first thought to hobo'in', hobo'in' / I took a freight train to be my friend, oh Lord' – imply that the hobo pretty soon changes his mind about whether the train is his friend, while his mother, who comes to say goodbye, also seems pretty definite about the disaster befalling her son:

Yes, my mother followed me that mornin', me that
mornin', boy
She followed me down to the yard, oh yeah
She said, 'My son he's gone, he's gone, he's gone
Yes, he's gone in a poorsome wear, oh yeah.'

As with Steve's own songs, this one is unusual in being in

the first person, and treating the plight of the hobo with some dignity, but there's still a sense that, in becoming a hobo, he's somehow becoming less than human.

When Steve sat down to write 'Hobo Blues' for *Cheap*, 'Hobo Low' for *Dog House Music*, and his other songs (and stories) that tell directly of the hard travelling life, he was doing something new. Where nearly everyone else, from Woody Guthrie to Bob Dylan, wrote about the hobo in the third person, as an alien creature, Steve presented a story from the hobo's point of view. He gave the hobo's account, and, though he didn't gloss over the difficulties of the life, Steve's hobo sounds like a real person. It seems that for the first time, the hobo had his own story, and his own dignity. He wasn't being looked down upon.

This is especially true of 'Hobo Low', which pulls no punches about the harsh realities of hobo life, but still creates a fleshed-out hobo character who isn't – as he is everywhere else – either pathetic, or a joke, or both, but a person we can picture, and believe in. The chorus of 'When you're hobo low there ain't nowhere to go / there ain't nuthin' lower than hobo low' leaves us in no doubt that this is a miserable lifestyle, but Steve also includes realistic details about the hobo's life, such as not being allowed to eat at the mission because 'The mission man said sorry boy you already been here twice this week', or the perils of a night's drinking: 'I drank ten whiskey bowls / Somebody bonk' me on the head and I woke up in a stinkin' hole'. Unlike most other hobos in the history of these songs, this is a real, fleshed-out character, with his own voice and his own story, not a stereotype to be pitied and patronised.

SEASICK STEVE

Whatever the truth of Steve's life as a hobo, being a brilliant musician, or any other kind of artist, isn't mainly about transcribing your own experiences, though that can sometimes be a starting point. It's about imagination: creating another world that the audience believes in and finds compelling. Steve has achieved that sympathetically and humanely, whereas a host of other famous songwriters could only sneer or patronise. The 'hobo' label has such a geographically specific history and culture, for British audiences at least, that it's easy to forget this has a contemporary relevance too. The number of people living rough in UK, at least, has been rising steadily for many years now. Steve's songs don't romanticise or distort the harsh realities of hobo life. They offer a dignified and convincing dramatic account of what that life might be like.

There's undoubtedly something great about Steve as a composer and performer. Taken altogether, he is a true original. He draws out the spirit of the old country blues, its gnarly, cracked sound, and its emotional directness, and he adds some of the power and anger of rock, and creates a sound audiences rightly love. There are traces of many predecessors in Seasick Steve – John Lee Hooker, R L Burnside, Junior Kimbrough, possibly ZZ Top too – but he is, to a remarkable extent, his own, original musician.

It's part of the tradition of the blues, of course, that musicians sing about their own troubles in a direct and personal way. As we've seen, Steve takes a creatively liberated attitude towards the traditions of the blues, almost always for the better. In terms of his attitude to his source material, he's more like a conceptual pop act. The great and original performers are the ones most likely to invent a persona for themselves. Think the Beatles and *Sgt. Pepper*, or any one of the kaleidoscope of roles invented by Madonna or David Bowie. There's more hobo in Steve than there is spaceman in Bowie, of course – but it's still a crafted persona.

Most of all, we learn some crucial and fascinating things about the essential ingredients of original artwork from Steve's life and the way in which he made music. It's more about poetic than literal truth: when Steve wrote his most explicitly hobo-themed lyrics there's no doubt that he was reflecting his experiences of being in ill health and suffering rejection in his professional career – even if it didn't reflect the way he'd actually spent eleven years of his life. And the most original creations often come from the darkest corners of the mind, in the most desperate moments of the creator's life.

CHAPTER 3

Growing Up in Oaklands

The established facts about Steve's early life are few and far between, and the sad story of the breakdown of his relationship with his stepfather, which forced him to run away some time between the ages of twelve and fourteen, is well known. More easily forgotten, and in some ways just as crucial for his later life, is the amazing and influential soundtrack of Steve's childhood. By his early twenties, when he went to France with his first wife, he had had personal experience of many of the most influential and important performers in both blues and rock'n'roll. He had seen the cutting edge of popular music change from the former to the latter, and understood how to blend the two for maximum impact.

Steve was born in the industrial port city of Oakland, California, on 19 March 1951, and he remained in the area until he ran away from his abusive stepfather in 1964 or

1965. His family was involved in the motor business, and his grandfather owned a repair garage. His original parents separated sometime around 1955, and his mother, who remained as Steve's main guardian and carer, married a Korean War veteran with a violent temper and a service revolver. Steve ran away from home to escape this violence, fearing that he might kill his stepfather if he stayed. His stepfather was many steps removed from his real parent. Most likely, he felt his family erode from under him, layer by layer, something that must surely have contributed to the sense of rootlessness that he has subsequently displayed, and the many places he has called home.

Mid-century Oakland was a growing city in an important strategic location, with both a shipping and rail terminus, in San Francisco Bay. From the point of view of Steve's upbringing, the city's most important features were its active music scene, its reputation for racial harmony and the fact that large numbers of labourers from the Deep South, both black and white, were recruited to work in its industrial plants during the 1940s.

Steve has commented on his early life only in snippets, leaving many details obscure. According to his oldest son, Sevrin, his original family, the Leaches, were not his true family. He was given away to them for adoption, but apparently Steve is Portuguese by birth. Sevrin reveals: 'He did learn that his real dad's last name was de Mello.' This is not as implausible as it sounds: in the 1950s, when Steve was born, the Portuguese community in Oakland was the largest in the USA. As famous navigators, the largest populations of Portuguese in the country have ended up in two of the country's most significant ports: Boston and Oakland. So it's entirely possible that Steve's birth parents were a Portuguese couple unable to look after him. However, adoption records in California are confidential, so, until Steve decides to tell his own life story, this is all we will be able to find out about his birth and immediate family.

Motor manufacture was Oakland's first big industry, emerging in the 1920s; with World War II, the city became the ideal location for both shipbuilding and canning. Until then, it had been a racially harmonious place. The Jim Crow segregation laws did not apply in the city, and until the war the black population was relatively small. It increased substantially during the 1940s as shipyard owner Henry J Kaiser recruited thousands of workers to build his wartime ship orders.

Most of these came from the Deep South, and both blacks and whites imported their racial attitudes from Alabama and Mississippi, which were more antagonistic than those of California. One notable feature of Steve's genre-bending musical style is the freedom with which he splices the mainly black music of the blues with the mainly white rock'n'roll. Steve's grandfather used to play music informally with the black musicians he employed, and this unusually open-minded, unhierarchical, laid-back vibe of home must have had some influence on Steve's attitude to both music and personal relationships.

One of thousands of black workers from rural Mississippi who moved to California to work in the naval dockyards was country blues guitarist and singer K C Douglas, who taught Steve his first guitar chords while he working at his grandfather's garage in the late 1950s. It doesn't seem to have been a very intensive process, and neither young Steve nor K C Douglas seems to have very committed to the learning process. In August 2007, Steve told Andy Gill from *The Independent*, 'I said I wanted to play guitar, so this old black guy who worked for my granddaddy, K C Douglas, he taught me how to play a few chords, which turned out to be blues chords.' Douglas (born in 1913) would have been under fifty at the time, so not that much of an old guy. Perhaps the young Steve was just exaggerating the appearance of even middle age, as young children tend to. Moreover, Douglas had had a hard life of manual labour, and possibly looked older than his years.

The most in-depth comment Steve has made about this time came in an early interview with the website bluesinlondon.com, published in March 2006 – before his *Hootenanny* breakthrough, but at a time when his act had already begun to gain some traction among blues fans:

> Well my grandfather had a car place in Oakland and during the war there was a big migration from Mississippi and Texas and Louisiana to Oakland to work in the shipyards or whatever, so there was lots of guys around at that time – Pee Wee Crayton, he worked in my gramps' shop! And my Dad played a boogie piano – he was a big boogie player, which was kinda rare for a white guy then. He played it before the war – I got 78's of him playing boogie in 1936 that I found when he died – so he was all over that shit.

Funny thing was though he didn't like black people! Well he did like 'em, sort of – he wanted to be a racist, but he was so nice it just didn't wash! If he was talking he'd say things like 'Them damn niggers' but then he'd hire them, and play music with them – he sent me to one, this old K C Douglas boy . . . K C, he'd talk about Tommy Johnson because they were buddies and they used to play down in Mississippi and he told me all these stories and taught me how to play the guitar a little bit.

I was eight or nine years old then, playing the guitar. My dad tried to teach me the boogie but I couldn't get my fingers apart . . . At the time I just thought guitars were something! Anyway, KC told me all them stories and got me all jacked up about the Delta, but it didn't sink in for a long time . . .

Pee Wee Clayton (born Connie Curtis Clayton) was originally from Texas, and played in a much smoother, shapelier way than Steve, so it would be difficult to argue that he was an early influence on him. By the time the young Steve would have met him, in the late 1950s, Clayton's number one in the *Billboard* R&B chart, 'Blues After Hours', was ten years behind him. It's sobering to reflect that both Clayton and Douglas had to work in the Leach family garage despite having released hit records.

Perhaps the most positive feature of this intriguing piece of social history is how racially tolerant the Leach household was, at last by the standards of the day. Steve's grandpa would presumably have been born towards the end of the nineteenth century, and there was no shortage of his compatriots of that generation who had no difficulty being racist at all. The garage sounds relaxed in terms of race relations, as was Oakland. That makes it less surprising than it would otherwise be that Steve's dad – and Steve too – played what was predominantly black music. Ironically, when things went wrong, Steve led what was in many respects the life of a homeless black musician.

K C Douglas must have had some influence over Steve, even if only as the source of the first guitar blues he heard. Douglas was one of the last great rural blues stylists. His career both tells us a lot about the changing social context of twentieth-century blues and offers some neat parallels with Steve's own career and interests. By the time he met Steve, Douglas had already recorded perhaps his most famous song, 'Mercury Boogie', which he wrote with Robert Geddins in 1948, about Mercury cars, a midmarket brand owned by the Ford Motor company. Musically, Douglas is more like Steve than Clayton, and it's worth considering his influence in a little more detail.

As a song, it's a simple, throwaway idea, which takes a traditional blues form, and turns it over to a modern subject, the automobile, which would have been a rarity where Douglas grew up, near Sharon, Mississippi, in the 1920s. So it may have been a way for him to reflect on the sudden changes in his life that came from the move from Mississippi to California – the song becomes a way for K C Douglas to unify, in a casual, rambling lyric, the traditional music in his life and the modern motor industry.

Given Steve's love of cars, it's tantalising to speculate

whether Douglas sang the song at work in the Leach family garage, and whether it had any impact on young Steve's interest. As Steve grew up in an automotive family, with someone like Douglas around singing about cars, some of the love must have rubbed off. Although Steve shows little affection for most of his childhood, it's notable that two of its distinctive features, his exposure to cars and the blues, are things that have remained important throughout his life, and became especially so just before his breakthrough, when the prospects for his musical career seemed most bleak.

'Mercury Boogie', later renamed 'Mercury Blues', has been covered by many performers, but by the time it really took off it was too late to help K C Douglas, who died in 1975 and never fully enjoyed the fruits of his success. Perhaps the most famous version of the song was by country singer Alan Jackson, a far slicker take with close-harmony choruses and production as smooth and gleaming as the hoods of the Mercury cars in the video.

Jackson's cover of the song was bought by Ford Motor Truck and used in an advertisement for its pickups in the 1990s, with the word 'Mercury' replaced by 'Ford truck'. The ad takes the song even further away from K C Douglas's plaintive, gritty original, with corporate lifestyle footage of waterskiing and shiny Ford trucks bouncing along in the dirt. By the time this ad was made, Douglas was long dead, and Steve Wold, as he was known by then, was hanging out on the liberal indie scene in Olympia, with garage rockers Murder City Devils and the punk band Fitz of Depression. Jackson's conservative country style was a long way behind him.

SEASICK STEVE

From the point of view of Steve's biography, however, the most interesting cover is by the Steve Miller Band, who covered it for their set at the Monterey International Pop Festival in 1967. Contrary to other aspects of Steve's life, we know for sure that he attended the festival. Miller's band also performed at Fillmore West in San Francisco earlier that year, supporting Chuck Berry, where they recorded the album *Live at the Fillmore Auditorium*. It's possible that the seventeen-year-old Steve Leach may also have been in the audience then.

Although K C Douglas never earned his entire living from music, he did have an active band, the Lumberjacks, and released albums on Downtown Records in Oakland from 1948. There was an active blues scene in the Bay Area at the time, thanks to the Southern workers drawn to Oakland's industry, and Douglas performed sporadically on it throughout the fifties and sixties. It's entirely feasible that, after he left home, Steve, who claims to have played with Son House and certainly did play with Lightnin' Hopkins, may have performed together with Douglas. Another regular on the Bay scene, and intriguing possible (though unproven) connection, who certainly performed at times with K C Douglas, is folk legend Jesse Fuller, who was slightly older than Douglas, and, like him, a refugee from the Deep South – Georgia, in Fuller's case.

There's no concrete evidence Steve knew Jesse Fuller personally, but circumstances suggest that it's likely. There's Steve's acquaintance with K C Douglas, and the fact they were both playing in the Bay Area music scene for some important years in the mid-1960s. In many respects, there are closer parallels between Steve's life and Fuller's, than that of Steve and K C Douglas. Like Steve, Fuller had had a rough childhood, with both birth parents and adoptive parents much worse than Steve's, if Fuller's various accounts are to be believed. He ran away from home early, without even the rudimentary musical education Steve had, and taught himself to play, developing his talent and repertoire himself, helped by impromptu encounters with older musicians at gigs.

The more specific resonances between the two as performers are intriguing. Both musicians have an easy charm and storytelling ability, and both make considerable use of improvised and homemade instruments, to the extent that they have become a kind of trademark. Fuller's most famous creation was his 'footdella', a six-string bass viol that he rigged up so he could play with one foot, while the other foot played cymbal, and a stand in front of him held a harmonica and kazoo. Fuller's music has a lighter, more genial and resigned mood than Steve's, but his independent, improvised tales of life on the road must have been somewhere in the back of Steve's mind when he wrote *Cheap*, and then, even more poignantly, *Dog House Music*, recorded mostly solo in his kitchen.

And there's another connection between Steve and Jesse Fuller. The Grateful Dead, formed nearby in Palo Alto just about the time Steve was leaving home, were Fuller fans, and covered two of his quirkier songs, 'Beat it on Down the Line', and 'The Monkey and the Engineer'. They are a good example of how musical ideas are passed on between two musicians who have, on the face of it, little in common. The country entertainer and pioneers of innovative psychedelia nonetheless shared a quirky sense of humour, which enabled them to see the potential in Fuller's songs to the benefit of both sets of musicians and, and above all, the incredibly rich West Coast music scene at the time.

Listening to the two versions side by side feels like a time-lapse experiment, so antiquated does Fuller's plaintive tone sound next to the Dead's full, juicy arrangement. Yet they both bring out the offbeat humour of a song about a man trying to get away from his job, with a similar lilting energy to the rhythm. They are father-and-son versions, with recognisable characteristics passed on, but also a clear sense of age separating them.

Bob Weir and Jerry Garcia of the Grateful Dead – which had initially formed as a jug band – had both been involved in the American Folk Revival of the late 1950s – as had, in a way, Jesse Fuller. They had then seen how Bob Dylan, the Beach Boys and others had transformed that sound using electronic instruments. This then led on, with a little more experimentation, to their attractively complex mature sound, drawn from so many traditional genres forged together in the new psychedelic age of mid-1960s San Francisco.

In an interview with Norwegian regional paper *Telen* from November 2000, shortly before Steve moved his family to Norway, he specifically singled out the Grateful Dead as a band he used to watch at the Fillmore in San Francisco. The transformation of popular music from K C Douglas and Jesse Fuller to bands like the Dead took place before Steve's eyes. With his diddley bow, 'Mississippi

Drum Machine' and other quaint pieces of musical heritage, he clearly understands the use and appeal of blues and folk traditions, but he also knows when a song needs the amped-up power of rock. It was a crucial period for his musical development, even though the world wouldn't see the results for nearly fifty years.

There are a few more glimpses of Steve's early engagement with music. Steve's earliest memory, recalled in many interviews, is sitting on the lap of his adoptive father at the piano while the older man played boogie-woogie. This happened many times, over several years, he says. In September 2008, he told Sean O'Hagan of *The Guardian*, 'Got a picture of me, just two years old, sitting on the old man's knee while he played the boogie. My dad loved that shit and I guess he passed some of it on to me.' Boogie-woogie was in his blood from the start. All the more appropriate that his breakthrough should come in a show hosted by Jools Holland, himself a boogie pianist of considerable ability.

Steve's first experience of the guitar came soon after. In an interview recorded in 2009 as part of BBC Four's *Bringing It All Home* season (and available on the BBC website), he recalls seeing his first guitar at the age of five or six on a summer camp. The camp had a stage for amateur performances, and Steve found a guitar there. It was his first contact with a real guitar. He says he's 'never seen nothin' more beautiful. I fell in love with the way it looked. That's when my daddy was trying to teach me the piano and I thought, no, no. I want me a guitar.' It's no exaggeration to say it was love at first sight, and the relationship begun that night has lasted longer than any other he has had, and has been at the centre of his life ever since.

Charles Perry's *Rolling Stone* feature about Steve's band Shanti throws up a little-known piece of information about his instrumental skills. In a paragraph about the band members' youthful experiences of music, Perry writes, 'Steve Leach (who had studied trombone) was running away from home in Oakland, at the age of twelve.' I have never found any other reference, anywhere, to Steve's study of the trombone, yet Perry spent at least a day with the band, speaking to them directly. Perhaps that's a surprise Steve is holding back for the next album.

Otherwise, the only events of Steve's early life that we know anything about are his parents' separation, the abuse from his new stepfather, and his final departure from home. The dates of the separation are prone to variation. In the same BBC interview he implies that his original father is still at home, trying to teach him boogie piano. Yet most of the versions of the split, given in various interviews, date it to when Steve was four, in 1955. It's clearly not a good idea to be too pedantic about the crucial dates in Steve's life. For someone whose youth was so itinerant, some of the details are bound to be blurred; it was only the musical experiences, especially those involving guitars, that burned into his memory.

The age Steve left home is twelve in some interviews, thirteen in some and fourteen in others. *Rolling Stone* (the account closest in time to the events themselves, and written at a time when Steve had less of an axe to grind) suggests he was twelve at the time and it was 1964, which would mean it took place right at the beginning of that year, before his birthday in March. If so, that would indeed give Steve a year or so to experience homelessness before the more interesting musical events kicked off over the bridge in San Francisco, from 1965 onwards.

The story runs like this, as told to Sean O'Hagan of *The Guardian* in September 2008:

> At thirteen, he had fled his home in Oakland, California, on the run from a violent stepfather who, in a fit of rage, had thrown him through the window of his mother's house. 'I had a moment of revelation,' he says. 'It was like I had been pushed right to the edge by what was happening to me, and I knew I was going to have to kill that motherfucker. Then, I suddenly thought: No, Steve, it don't have to be like that. You don't have to end up in jail for one reckless act. It suddenly hit me that there was another way out. I could just run, and keep running. That way, at least my life would be my own.'

He tells the same story in 'Dog House Boogie', from 2006: 'Now my mom an' dad broke up when I was four years old / When I was seven she went and got herself another man; it was hell, y'all / I left home 'fore I was fourteen years of age; I figured I'd do better on my own'. Strangely, some of the life story in the rest of the song we know isn't true, but this part matches everything else he's said, so it probably is.

SEASICK STEVE

There's far less certainty about where Steve went next, a question that we will examine in the next chapter. The important thing to remember about this stage in Steve's life is that it was steeped in the blues. For the next thirty-five years, he was mostly working in rock music of one form or another, though he did do some backing work for bluesmen such as Lightnin' Hopkins. But rock'n'roll was about to flower, catching Steve at the most impressionable age, and right on his doorstep. It's fair to say it took over his life. Somewhere at the back of Steve's musical memory, however, the vibe, the feel, the techniques of the blues remained alive. It comes through in his love of lo-fi, analogue recording equipment, for which he later scoured the States when equipping the studio he built in Olympia in the 1990s, and later moved, along with his family, to Norway. Most of all, of course, it comes through in his own music.

It seems strange that he comes back to this music and these experiences only at this stage in his life, in his mid-fifties, when he'd been working with much more contemporary sounds such as grunge and indie rock for more than a decade. Yet this stage in his life is a classic example of the blues experience. When he moved to Norway in 2001, taking his lovingly assembled studio with him, he seemed to be planning a continuation of the professional life he'd had in Olympia, but in the more amenable circumstances of Norway, close to his wife's family and (apparently an important factor for Steve) away from George W Bush's crass and belligerent America.

The studio had been a success in Olympia, but,

for reasons we'll look at later, didn't really take off commercially in Notodden (though it's still working, part of the new Blues Senter and Blueseum in the town). He'd started performing with local band the Level Devils partly, it's said, as a way of earning money to replace what he wasn't making at the studio, though that avenue hadn't – yet – really worked out either. By the time he wrote *Dog House Music*, he'd had a heart attack, the band had dispersed and he'd sold his final share in the studio at a massive loss. He recorded the album on a four-track he retrieved from the studio, the only piece left from the gear he'd spent so long assembling. It was a classic blues moment: just when so much of Steve's professional life seemed to be falling in around his ears, he looked into his heart, picked up his guitar and told his story.

Dog House Music is full of bleak, cold, lonely stories. Steve isn't really singing about his problems at that time. It was his musical career that had gone wrong in Notodden, not his personal life: he was surrounded by close family. So the solitary man in 'Salem Blues', thinking about the girl he treated unkindly, and the raw hobo's life in 'Hobo Low' don't literally tell us what was happening to Steve at this time. But they do tell us about his mood, and that, when he needed to focus his pain, he turned to the blues.

Of course, the timing could hardly be more ironic. Just at the moment when he sounds so low, he was only a few months away from his life-changing appearance on *Later* . . . When Steve left home in 1964 or 1965, he left behind an environment full of the blues, and largely exchanged it for one where rock was the dominant music. But the music and the message of the blues stayed in his heart and in his mind, and in his blood, and came back to him when he most needed it.

Steve has, in public, anyway, had a love/hate relationship with the blues, and has often spoken of the music in the same way one might describe an old uncle: someone with embarrassing views and bad breath, whom one feels obliged to visit, and who might even help one out financially, but who still needs to be kept safely out of sight. What Steve says about the unpopularity of the blues is often exaggerated. For example, in November 2009, he made these remarks in Neuland Concerts' press release about *Man From Another Time*:

> The country blues was getting to be a dead issue in America. It had a brief revival in the early Sixties when they dug up those old Mississippi guys. But pretty soon they was back workin' in the train station, or deliverin' the laundry.

This was of the case for some bluesmen, certainly. It was approximately true of K C Douglas, for example, who did work other jobs while singing. Jesse Fuller made a living as a musician, however, while John Lee Hooker recorded with Canned Heat, appeared in the cult 1980 movie *The Blues Brothers* and opened a nightclub in San Francisco called John Lee Hooker's Boom Boom Boom. Son House, meanwhile, would have supported himself comfortably from his touring in later life had he not been quite so determined to drink away his earnings.

In fact, after the initial blues recording boom of the 1920s – which uncovered the first generation of blues stars such as Mamie Smith, Ma Rainey and W C Handy, followed later in the decade by the plaintive country sound of Blind Lemon Jefferson – the Depression and the World War II interrupted the growth of the music. But the new, college-based scene for authentic roots music in the fifties revived the careers of the surviving first generation, and the most successful, such as Son House, carried on performing for the rest of their lives. By the sixties, however, even though some of the individuals had retired or been sidelined, blues was the backbone of popular music. At Monterey, both Janis Joplin and Jimi Hendrix launched their careers as mainstream stars playing blues covers.

Steve's main – and cannily strategic – concern seems really to have been less about the blues in themselves, and more about being pigeonholed in a small and ageing musical clique, without the opportunity to reach a new and younger audience. In March 2006, he confessed to bluesinlondon.com:

> . . . when I heard those bands like the Steve Miller Blues Band, or the Santana Blues Band, or the Paul Butterfield Blues Band, I really liked them, but that wasn't the blues for me . . . I'd grown up with blues since I could remember and they were all different. So I came backwards, I very much wanted to do all that stuff, but I got gigs playing the blues because I could play it, like in the folky kind of way, and not many people could do it that way then. But that

didn't last very long – I got real unpopular . . . I didn't have no job!

In other words, he played country blues because he was the only one who could do it, even though he would have played a more modern take on the genre if he could. And it was still unpopular. The same kind of diffidence, and standoffishness, was displayed when he discussed the blues with Thomas H Green of *The Arts Desk*:

> I'd never thought about my music being the blues. When I was a kid there weren't all these lines. Some real black music came under 'Race records' but in general it was all kind of mixed up. I never thought of myself as a blues person. When I was a kid, blues people were black people living on a farm or something. I always thought I played hillbilly music. You know what? When no one's listening you don't need to reflect too much on what you play because no one's asking . . . The one time I thought about it was when I got asked to play a couple of songs with [the late Mississippi bluesman] R L Burnside in 1996. Someone said, 'We need someone who knows how to play old-style blues.' I thought, 'Do I play that kind of music?' It was the first time I reflected on it but nothing more happened until I was in England and people were saying, 'You play the blues', and I was, like, 'Wow! Do I?'

This seems to be a case of protesting too much. It's not

credible that a man who has spent his entire life at least on the fringes of the professional music business shouldn't know what music he's playing, even if he does play a mixture of genres. He must also have known that, when he was a kid, most blues musicians had already left the farms and were working in places like his grandpa's garage – after all, one of them taught him the guitar.

The trouble is, whether Steve likes it or (as he claims) not, his life has been run through with the blues in all sorts of ways that still reverberate in his music. Steve's restlessness, throughout his adult life, is another time-honoured characteristic of a blues singer. And, when he decided to move his whole family out of America, home of the blues, to Europe, he settled on a town – Notodden – with a thriving blues festival. Shortly before Steve left the USA, Curtis Andreen – drummer with the Tremens – noted in an interview on a site called *Ear Pollution*: 'We were going to go on tour with him, then he found out there was this huge blues scene in Norway and ended up moving there.' It's unusual to move your whole family to another continent for a music scene you don't like – although the move was also reportedly his Norwegian wife's decision, at least in part. We get a completely different picture of Steve's attitude to the blues from an account he gives to the Notodden newspaper *Telen* in November 2000, as he describes his plans to move his family, and also his studio, to Notodden.

Blues music has always been central to my soul. Having dragged myself half way round the world, it was amazing to discover that people in Notodden feel the same. Until the meeting in Notodden I had not really thought about bringing my big studio over here. But the more I talked to Jostein [Forsberg, Notodden music festival director] and the festival management the more I realised that this studio fitted perfectly into the plans to create a European Blues Centre.

At the time he was, of course, selling himself to the musical community of Notodden. He had a studio to launch, and emphasising his love of the blues was only good business sense. Yet it's still quite hard to swallow the change from the blues being 'central to my soul' to something he didn't even know he was playing. In the UK at least, the ultra-traditional, core blues community has a reputation for an obsessive regard for the technical rules of song-composition, and for an original, genre-straddling songwriter like Steve, being too closely associated with them would not help his popularity. All the same, it's clear that his feelings for the blues, as with his feelings for other aspects of his life, have sometimes been conveniently shaped according to his audience.

Sean O'Hagan explains Steve's relationship with blues and modern audiences well in his September 2008 piece for *The Guardian*:

It says something about the times we live in that Seasick Steve has managed to slip, mostly by word-of-mouth success, through into the mainstream. In doing so, he has become a hero to a generation for whom the word 'hobo' is about as meaningless as the word 'blues'. What they see in him is something that's long gone, something they can only ever experience vicariously through the rough energy of his songs.

Refreshingly, the object of their devotion doesn't give a hoot about 'authenticity', and rejects the loaded term 'blues singer' outright. 'I'm an entertainer,' he says. 'I tell stories but my stories are real. I give one hundred per cent of myself every time I walk onto a stage. Don't matter if it's ten people or ten thouand, I want to make them remember me.'

Eventually, Steve broke through into the mainstream in dramatic fashion, although I'm not sure it was by accident so much as by deliberately avoiding the traditional blues audience, which he knows full well is very limited in reach and appeal. It's a very effective strategy, as is the way he tries to make sure people remember him. And the reality of his stories? His approach here too is very strategic.

There is probably the heritage of both the authentic bluesman and the street performer in his approach to being an 'entertainer'. One telling phrase he often uses about himself is 'song-and-dance man', an idea that he describes here, in his 2006 interview with bluesinlondon.com which sounds plausibly like something a busker, or original juke-joint blues musician, would have created:

SEASICK STEVE

> Well I only can play instinctively – I don't got all that
> fancy stuff. But I'll tell you one thing that I learnt . . .
> For me the story was always the important thing, or
> the entertainer thing – I was a song and dance man!
> This playing the guitar fancy, that don't help you on
> the street. You gotta make like a song and dance and
> be loud and shit. All the boys that I ever talked to,
> the guitar was real secondary.

Even a hobby like his love of cars comes in many ways from
the blues. Both Steve's family history and the history of the
blues are crammed full of automobiles. Steve's grandfather
owned a garage. Steve's first guitar lesson was with a
musician, K C Douglas, whose breakthrough song was
about cars. Steve's first professional tour (probably) was
with Lightnin' Hopkins, a man who also wrote several well-
known songs about cars, such as 'Automobile Blues' and
'Lightnin's Discourse on the Cadillac'. There was Robert
Johnson's 'Terraplane Blues', Chuck Berry's 'Maybellene',
and so on. Cars and the blues are inseparable, so, when
Steve talks to *Top Gear*'s Jeremy Clarkson about his old
cars, he is working within something of a well-established
tradition for blues singers. Automobiles and the blues were
born and came to maturity at around about the same time,
and many blues musicians travelled from the South to
work in the car factories around Detroit.

Steve's family life has a rich vein of the blues running
through it, too. While his violent home life and early
departure from his household is abnormal for a middle-
class white boy in 1960s suburbia, it's a familiar element

in the biography of many a black blues singer. John Lee Hooker ran away from home when he was fourteen. Jesse Fuller was abused and neglected by an adoptive family, who sent him to work breaking rocks in a quarry as a child, until he too had had enough and ran away. Frankie Lee Sims from Texas, singer of 'Lucy Mae Blues' – and Lightnin' Hopkins's cousin – ran away from home at the age of twelve to become a musician.

The tough family, the rejection, the poverty, the nomadic lifestyle and the busking, with music-making providing a means to earn a basic living on the road – all these are classic elements of a blues singer's backstory. The blues – especially in the raw, improvised form that K C Douglas sang and taught Steve in his grandfather's garage – initially evoked the safety of home. And, when that crucial security was taken away from him as a child, the blues became the ideal means of expression for Steve's sorrow and rootlessness.

CHAPTER 4

San Francisco 1965-72: The Bass With the Macramé Tassel

The first big puzzle of Steve's life occurs when he ran away from home. Until that point, all sources are agreed on where he lived, even if we don't know a huge amount about what his life was like. We've already seen that, according to Steve's chronology, the moment he left home was the beginning of his 'eleven years bumblin'' around', but according to his version of events it happened ten years before it actually did – because Steve was already on record as having been in Haight-Ashbury, San Francisco, in the mid-1960s. And what self-respecting teenage musician would leave Haight-Ashbury to go and ride trains?

Clarksdale, Mississippi, the centre of blues singing – and the town Steve would use, nearly forty years later in Norway, as the given address of his record company There's A Dead Skunk Records – is more than two thousand miles from Oakland, California, and the home he ran away from. It had little to offer a young musician, even one interested in the blues. By 1965, most of the early pioneers and the names we now associate with the breakthrough of Mississippi blues in around 1930 had died (Robert Johnson) or had moved away (Son House, Howlin' Wolf) and were busy touring.

In 1965, in California, there were much more influential destinations for a young musician, which were also much closer to home – right on Steve's doorstep, in fact. The place Steve ended up would influence his music for the rest of his life – and was home to some of the pivotal events in the history of popular music. Between 1965 and 1967, California was home to the birth of the hippie revolution, the Summer of Love and the Monterey Pop Festival. Steve was present at all of them. How do we know he was there, aside from the overwhelming circumstantial evidence? As luck would have it, he has said so himself, although not since he became 'Seasick Steve'.

In addition to the account in *Rolling Stone*, which suggests Steve left home early in 1964 at the age of twelve, confirmation of his whereabouts comes in an interview with Norwegian newspaper *Telen*. This has followed the arrival and intriguing career of this exotic American musician with great interest for the past sixteen years. In an article by Knut H Slettemo, published on 13 November 2000, the writer comments,

It was inevitable that Steve ended up being an active musician and record producer. The impact of having an address in Haight-Ashbury, San Francisco, as a teenager, from 1965 to 1967, would always be considerable. This was the right time and the right place for people who like rock music. It was the USA's most important hippie centre, and any band worth mentioning from the Sixties played there and hung out at a collective. Steve did not immediately understand what he was involved in: 'I was at Fillmore and saw bands playing almost daily. There were local bands like The Grateful Dead, The Doors, Janis Joplin, etc. In '67 I hitchhiked out to Monterey Pop Festival and saw the concert where Jimi Hendrix set fire to his guitar. Only in retrospect did I realise how lucky I was to see all this.'

In January 2009, Steve told a rather different story to *The Daily Mail*: 'The whole Haight-Ashbury scene was crazy,' he said. 'You didn't need money. You could sleep in people's houses and there always seemed to be free food around. But if you stayed in San Francisco too long, you lost touch with reality and the rest of the country. I didn't stick around.'

So either he was at Fillmore almost daily, or he just dropped in briefly for the experience – which? His later comments are associated with a Seasick Steve PR programme that involved a lack of clarity over his age. The earlier remarks also seem more likely for a young guitarist, and we can be almost entirely sure, for reasons I will come to later, that this is the correct version. Who wants 'the rest of the country' when you have the Grateful Dead and Janis

Joplin on your doorstep – and can even, as Steve told *Uncut* magazine in June 2009, be 'a friend of Janis Joplin from a spell in mid-Sixties San Francisco'?

Oakland is just a couple of miles over the Bay Bridge from San Francisco, and the Haight-Ashbury district is right in the middle of that city, its name taken from the name of the two roads that cross at its centre. San Francisco had been a Beat destination since the mid-1950s, the city's reputation as a centre for counterculture initially established by poets such as Lawrence Ferlinghetti, founder of City Lights Booksellers and Publishers. The Six Gallery – the location of a famous reading in October 1955 that featured Allen Ginsberg (presenting his poem 'Howl' for the first time) and Michael McClure among others, and which established the public presence of the Beat Generation in the city – was at 3119 Fillmore Street, only a short distance from the concert venue where Steve spent so much time ten years later.

That San Francisco should become the centre of musical counterculture was in many ways a natural evolution, and the establishment scarcely noticed the transformation from beatnik to hippie, although the movement that was born in Haight-Ashbury during these years went beyond the beatniks, embracing and affecting a far wider tranche of society. Steve did meet some beatniks, though his view of them was chequered, and seemed to imply they were not the authentic voice of protest music. In June 2011, he told Thomas H Green of *The Arts Desk*:

> I met beatniks in San Francisco. They hung out on
> North Beach and they was into jazz – cool, daddio,

THE BASS WITH THE MACRAMÉ TASSEL

they had goatees and turtlenecks. They was older too, in their thirties and forties back then, thirty-five in 1966. They listened to poetry and someone playing the saxophone. That was not my scene. Never, ever did I meet one of these fuckers on the road, no students, just people who something had happened in their lives, problems with the police, lost their family, drinking, them guys from the war who never fit back in.

Haight-Ashbury was a working-class neighbourhood in the early 1960s, and accommodation was cheap and plentiful – something that must have attracted the fourteen-year-old runaway Steve Leach, who had nowhere else to go. It would be fascinating to hear the first-hand thoughts of this aspiring young guitarist who had happened, really just by chance, upon this extraordinary renaissance of a new kind of music, allied to what were considered at the time even more important campaigns for expanded states of consciousness, and radical political change.

LSD, born originally of 1950s CIA experiments into mind control, was a central part of the movement's exploration of alternative states of mind, and was legal until 1966; marijuana was also widespread. Originally a destination for those committed to the cause, Haight-Ashbury experienced what is best described as a blossoming 1966 and 1967, dying away after the Summer of Love.

Clearly, Steve had a lot of fun in Haight-Ashbury. Transplant almost any teenage boy from a violently repressive home into a commune of free food, drugs and

love, and fun is the likely outcome. As he told bluesinlondon.
com in 2006:

> I didn't totally understand what was going on there
> at the time, but there was lots of free places to sleep
> and lots of girls, and it was real nice! I really liked it.
> But I just happened to come back to San Francisco
> at that time without knowing something was
> going on. I'd heard you could go over to this place
> Haight-Ashbury – I didn't know exactly what they
> was doing, but they had free food, and love and
> everything, so it was all good! I had a great time . . .

We can dispute the phrase 'I just happened to come back
to San Francisco at that time', because he must have
come directly from home in Oakland. It's even possible
that rumours of this musicians' commune with free
accommodation may have encouraged him to leave home
when he did, though we have no reason to doubt that the
atmosphere with his stepdad was genuinely nasty.

For Steve, what mattered most about Haight-Ashbury
was the immersion in the company and practice of
professional musicians. Had his childhood been happier,
it's possible he would, like his father and grandfather,
have become a garage owner who played a bit on the side.
Moving to San Francisco when he did gave him company
and training, as both a performer and an engineer, and
guaranteed that he would be a musician for the rest of his
life. The profile in *Telen*, written when Steve was keen to
impress a new audience with his musical credentials, is

quite correct to point out that his time in Haight-Ashbury made a musical career inevitable.

The psychedelic music characteristic of Haight-Ashbury seems so far removed from Seasick Steve's style today that we might assume there would be no influence on him. In the documentary *Haight-Ashbury in the Sixties*, Paul Kantner of Jefferson Airplane described the music of the period as deriving from a 'culture semi-immersed in acid'. There were other ways of achieving a state of heightened consciousness, however, and Steve did show an interest in some of those, which shows him to be a true son of the Summer of Love. Today, of course, a growling realism, so up-close you can see skin hair bristle, is one of Steve's trademarks, but there are ways of incorporating all sorts of influences into that.

However, there was one famous Haight-Ashbury musician – the one Steve knew best – who does serve as something as a template for his own later solo career. As he would himself, Janis Joplin took the blues, electrified them and made the songs utterly unmistakable with a voice of raw, spine-tingling power. Like Steve, she sings about people living lives on the edge – with quivering passion or explosive rage. Like Steve, she exhibits fantastic vocal control over whole scope of the voice, from the most delicate whisper to the most abrasive howl. In the lower and middle of the range, there's the same intimacy, and at full stretch she can out-howl any wolf. Listening to Joplin's most raw and most fervent performances – 'Ball and Chain', 'To Love Somebody' and 'Work Me, Lord' are a good place to start – there's a sense with both singers that we're getting a close-up of their tonsils, and, just behind that, the beating heart. Lyrically and thematically, there's occasionally some overlap (as, to be fair, you'd expect with two blues singers). On 'Me and Bobby McGee', Joplin sings, 'Freedom is just another word for nothing left to lose' – a sentiment with just the right amount of sardonic fatalism to fit into any number of Seasick Steve pieces. She doesn't tend to weave her hurt into humour, or self-deprecation, or long, shaggy stories, as he does, but both are instantly unique and recognisable, with brilliantly theatrical projection of their raw, desperate passion. Steve was writing thirty-five years after Joplin's death, but it's touching to think that she was still inspiring her friend's original work so long after that.

Joplin didn't fit in at all in her conservative hometown of Port Arthur, Texas, and she, like Steve, had found kindred spirits in the musical community in Haight-Ashbury. She had suffered what today would be regarded as spiteful misogynistic abuse, voted 'Ugliest Man on Campus' while at university in Texas. Although their circumstances were superficially different, psychologically the two artists went through similar ruts: in 2003, Steve was also isolated, demeaned, and, feeling threatened for his musical future, reached into himself and created a howling blast of pain that couldn't be anyone else.

It should be noted that Joplin lived in San Francisco in 1963–5, returning to Texas in May 1965 (only two months after Steve's fourteenth birthday) because her health was suffering. She returned to San Francisco in June 1967, and it must have been in this second spell that she got to know Steve, who would by then have had time to find his feet in the musical scene. She was in a relationship with Country Joe McDonald for about three months in 1967, and he shared her flat in a now-iconic house (it was the address listed on her driving licence) at 122 Lyon Street; after McDonald left she shared with friend and clothing designer Linda Gravenites, moving to Noe Street in April 1968 for more space. (Despite having broken through by then, she still couldn't afford her own place.) Steve would have seen her perform at Monterey in June 1967, where she sang in a breakthrough gig with the band Big Brother and the Holding Company.

According to Ed Vuillamy, in a long, retrospective piece for *The Guardian* entitled 'Love and Haight', Joplin was the 'empress' of the Summer of Love. He quotes Sam Andrew, her guitarist with Big Brother and the Holding Company: '"Janis," sighs Andrew, "was the most talented person on the scene. But why is it always the same? Edith Piaf. Billie Holiday. The drugs, the drink, the wrong man – all this passion, at a cost of self-destruction?"' He continues,

Janis used to ride around town on a Vespa. She loves Edith Piaf. I remember an afternoon in 1963 when Piaf died, she listened to 'Non, Je ne regrette rien' over and over. 'Let me put it on just one more time, just one last time' . . . [Janis] knows how to laugh. She's funnier than 10 people . . . [Country] Joe and Janis used to have violent arguments about politics. He couldn't understand that it was political of her just to stand on the stage. She mistrusted the politically inclined.

And Andrew is eloquent on the decline of Haight-Ashbury, too, as its ideals became corrupted by that persistent vandal of idealism: money. 'Yes, of course, we all got record contracts,' he noted, 'but whatever it was, it was over, that moment of grace. There was the Monterey Pop festival in June, and all the kids came up to fill the Haight. With them, the vultures moved in. What we had done was commercialised. People moved in who wanted to make a buck out of it all, especially the drugs. Hard drugs arrived – speed, meth, cocaine, heroin. The drugs became tiring and boring. And free love? Women were raped – it became a perversion of what it had been before.' By the autumn of 1967, most of the kids who'd just come to try the scene were heading home for college, in some case singed by the experience.

Andrew's description of the approach to music prevalent in Haight-Ashbury could also apply to Steve, both as producer and performer. 'That was the time,' Andrew recalled, 'when we lived our lives as musicians rather than people with a career in music. Ourselves, the Dead, Airplane and Quicksilver. We in Big Brother wanted to be Indians, tribal, while Quicksilver wanted to be the cowboys, with their boots, carrying rifles around.' The idea of music as vocation, as lifestyle, is something Steve lived very fully for nearly thirty years after the Summer of Love, until his breakthrough in 2006.

Steve's claim to have been friends with Joplin is based on his claim to have been ten years older than he was; in fact, when he met her, he'd have been only sixteen, and pretty green, given he'd only two years earlier left the completely different environment of home. Yet if he could play guitar, and make himself useful at gigs and rehearsals – and he could probably do both those things – it's a plausible friendship, and it shows how well established he was in the scene. Being a shrewd and diplomatic pair of ears was a skill he made a living from much later, in Olympia.

As it turns out, one of the broader philosophical agendas taking place at Haight-Ashbury was essential for Steve's musical and personal development, and remained so for at least fifteen years. There's little sign that he took up with, or showed an interest in, the philosophy behind actor Pete Coyote's proto-anarchistic Digger Movement, for example, which took its inspiration from the English seventeenth-century revolutionaries, although he did enjoy their free food, as he told Thomas H Green of *The Arts Desk*, in June 2011: 'These people called the Diggers would come and feed you for free. They'd bring this soup truck onto the pan-handle there and, miraculously, food would show up. Peter Coyote was one of them. Everything was a little bit magic there.'

Author and LSD advocate Ken Kesey and his Merry Pranksters in their psychedelic school bus frequently appeared as jolly provocateurs on the scene, supporting events such as the Love Pageant Rally, which took place on 6 October 1966 – the day that California made LSD illegal. This event was masterminded by the founders of the *San Francisco Oracle*, Allen Cohen and Michael Bowen, and was billed as a celebration of innocence and transcendental consciousness, involving exuberant costumes, much incense and communal acid-taking as culmination. Bigger events with similar principles followed, such as the Human Be-In in January 1967 – at which Timothy Leary told everyone to 'turn on, tune in and drop out' – and the Summer of Love soon after.

Steve's attitude to drugs is pretty uncomplicated. It would have been impossible to miss them around at Haight-Ashbury. Realistically, he must have done them too, though it's not something he talks about often, and seems to be able to enjoy himself without any danger of addiction. In June 2011, he told Thomas H Green of *The Arts Desk*: 'I feel sorry for people who fuck it up. I'm really lucky because I've never had the hook. Some people can take one drink and they're fucked. I've done hard drugs, shit like that, even smoking cigarettes, and I didn't have the hook, I could just stop so I was born lucky that way.'

For many sixties musicians – most famously the Beatles – experiments with drugs led to exploration of another kind of mind-bending. We know for certain that Steve not only took part in Transcendental Meditation, but also became influential in promoting its beliefs through music. The Beatles first met the movement's leader, Maharishi Mahesh Yogi, in 1967, when he was on a lecture tour in London, then went to the Welsh town of Bangor to hear him talk again. Thereafter, the group decided to learn more about meditation, and travelled to the Maharishi's retreat in Rishikesh, India, to do so. The encounter was not wholly successful, though, and the band left earlier than planned, with some reports suggesting a rift between them and the guru.

However, their involvement gave the movement

immensely valuable publicity, and credibility within the musical community. Transcendental Meditation was just beginning to take root in the Bay Area around 1967, and this part of the USA has remained one of the most important centres for the practice. By 1970, a course in TM entitled 'Science of Creative Intelligence' was introduced at Stanford University in Palo Alto, and apparently attracted the largest undergraduate enrolment of any course ever taught at that institution.

According to Allan Kozinn, writing in the *New York Times* in February 2008, there were health benefits to Transcendental Meditation, which also applied in large measure to substantial sections of the Haight-Ashbury community. 'At the time,' he notes, 'The Beatles, especially Lennon and Harrison, were still trying to tap into the cosmic subconscious, or eternity, or whatever, by using LSD. The maharishi's transcendental meditation techniques promised to get them there without the chemicals.'

So how do we know Steve was involved in Transcendental Meditation? It's actually the most clearly substantiated episode of this part of his life, and there are, amazingly, both photos and a video as proof – for it was all tied up with his joining a band. The period we can document with certainty lasted from 1970 until 1972, but, for Steve to be in a position to take part in 1970, he must have been around the Bay Area, actively participating in Transcendental Meditation for a couple of years beforehand, in order to be chosen. The band was called Shanti, and it was a collaboration between Indian musicians Zakir Hussain (tabla, dholak and naal), Aashish Khan (sarod) and Pranhesh Khan (tabla and naal), and Americans Neil Seidel (lead guitar), Steve Haehl (lead vocal and guitar), Frank Lupica (drums) and Steve Leach – as he was known then – on bass guitar. If anyone doubts that this Steve Leach is Seasick Steve, music writer Richie Unterberger removes all uncertainty in his notes: 'Bassist Steve Leach has reinvented himself as the blues musician Seasick Steve . . .' The use of the word 'reinvented' is suggestive. Fortunately for Steve's fans, the band's self-titled album, originally released in 1971, was rereleased in 2015 on Real Gone Music, with some very illuminating liner notes by Unterberger, who explains:

> Even in an era when eclecticism flourished in rock, Shanti had an unlikely combination of diverse backgrounds. As lead guitarist Neil Seidel explains, Zakir Hussain . . . and sarod player Aashish Khan . . . wanted to form some kind of popular fusion group, because they wanted to showcase the beauty of Indian music and promote it to the world. They wanted it to be sort of like a mainstream pop thing, with an Indian hook. From what I perceived from Aashish at the time, he realised the necessity of making it accessible.

So there was an evangelical quality to the Indian musicians' involvement, wishing to share their traditions in a popular format. What about the motives of the other band members? Neil Seidel explains in the album notes: 'All of the American musicians in the group were initiates of Transcendental Meditation. The song lyrics were all somewhat spiritual in nature. While the Indian musicians' agenda was by and large to promote Indian music to the non-Indian world, the Americans saw Shanti as a way to promote "Consciousness" – meditation etc through music.'

Zakir Hussain expanded on this theme in an interview on *The Jake Feinberg Show* (a programme of musical interviews) recorded in 2012, and related in Unterberger's album notes. The band's religious outlook was steeped throughout their work. There was obviously nothing remotely opportunistic about Steve's interest in Transcendental Meditation. Hussain explained,

> It worked out in a way, where six people came into the room of like-minded nature. Because those four were already following the spiritual nature of meditation and stuff . . . and were involved in yoga, and meditative practices. And then were also listening to Indian music day in and day out. So for them to listen to Aashish and me playing was just like coming home, or seeing visually what they had already been experiencing through records and tapes and films and stuff and so on. Some somehow the six of us were brought together. It was just like the right mix of people in the same room, and the people who wanted to interact with each other, share with each other, and be friends with each other, live together, eat together, cook together and whatnot. And all that had somehow seeped into the music as well. So it just somehow felt right. A family had come together, and that's what it's all about.

For Steve, then, coming home was 'to listen to Aashish and me playing' Indian music. If only the BBC had known that when they made the documentary *Bringing It All Back Home*. They bewildered poor Steve, taking him round Mississippi when he'd have felt much more at home listening to Indian music and meditating! Seriously, however, this is a beautiful account of a unity that's fairly rare in rock music history. And it demonstrates beyond any doubt that Steve was a committed Transcendental Meditator by this time and for presumably years beforehand, so much so that he joined a band to promote those ideas. It seems, then, the philosophical side of Haight-Ashbury had much more influence on him than he has previously admitted. And it's very likely, although not provable, that Transcendental Meditation remained an important part of Steve's life (and, later, that of his family) for at least the next twenty years, as we shall see.

In what's sometimes interpreted as a final attempt to get Shanti another record deal, they were given a full-page feature in the 25 May 1972 issue of *Rolling Stone*. Charles Perry accompanied the band to a gig at the Lion's Share in San Anselmo, Marin County, then home together afterwards. The published piece is more important for the wonderful hippie atmosphere it evokes than in establishing any more facts about Steve's life, though it does confirm some details. In addition to the extra information about his early departure from home, it also verifies that 'Steve Leach was also in meditation class' (along with everyone else in the band) when Shanti formed in October 1970. Their album was recorded in September 1971.

There are endearing cosmetic details. Steve has a 'bass with the macramé tassel', which he plays for the gig. The atmosphere between players is appealingly zany, as this exchange between Zakir Hussain (tabla) and Steve suggests:

> 'Listen, I've got a new melody part for just before the break, you know it, diggy diggy diggy dah, didah? It goes like this,' and he sang: 'Kit kidiggy nigdat kiddy kidiggy kiddy kiniggidat dat dat kidat kinnidinny dig dinny dig diggy dig kidiggy kidinnidinndat.'
>
> 'I don't know, Zakir,' said the lean blond bassist [Steve], with a studied look at his folded hands, 'if we can learn that in time for the next set.'

Perry's description of the gig Shanti plays confirms that this is 'psychedelic music', and describes their 'San Francisco Sound' as an 'Indian melodic line, reborn as a rock & roll riff'. Time to revise our judgement, then, about whether Steve was influenced by psychedelic music, even if it is difficult to see how he fits it into his current act.

Food was an important part of the band's philosophy too:

> Dinner at the Shanti house was what you might expect: organic and curried. 'Music, food and philosophy – that's what we were going to adopt as our band motto,' said Neal. Philosophy, yes: the Americans in the band are all meditators, as the

simple, spacey sentiments about life and love they sing might indicate, and the band almost toured at one point with Swami Satchidananda [Indian religious teacher, spiritual master and yoga guru]. They feel a certain incongruity about playing in the dance halls and even bars they've been booked into.

Best of all, though, is this casual intervention:

'Hey,' said Steve Leach, poking his head into the room, 'I've had this deep insight about the group. All our drummers were breast-fed and all the guitarists were bottle-fed.' Zakir [Hussain, tabla player] grinned and whipped out a rattle of beats on the floor with his hands.

Spoken like a down-home hobo.

One of the bands often mentioned by pre-Seasick Steve and those close to him are the Beach Boys, and it's possible, if not likely, that his contact with them came via the Transcendental Meditation community. Brian Wilson wrote the soppy 'TM Song', their most explicit musical reference to TM, released on the 1976 album *15 Big Ones*, but the influence goes back much earlier. Mike Love told *The Portland Tribune* in February 2013,

We met Maharishi Mahesh Yogi in Paris in 1967 and he taught us the technique. It's meant to be practised twice a day, morning and evening. It's such a great thing. You sleep the night and get up the next morning and you feel completely rested. When you meditate, all those feelings of grogginess and irritation and fatigue are eliminated. Your biochemistry changes. It's very simple but amazing stuff.

Late 1967 also saw the demise of the Summer of Love, and the effective end of the Haight-Ashbury hippie community that had so quickly arisen. It makes sense that, as one consciousness-expanding focus gave way, the remaining musical community should settle on another one. For young musicians such as Steve, especially those who largely relied on fellow musicians to be family as well as friends, the attraction of something such as TM is obvious and understandable. We cannot prove definitively that Steve was involved in this spiritual discipline from 1967, but given the situation with Shanti, and his obvious commitment to the cause, it seems highly likely.

Clearly, the hippie scene had a political influence on Steve. As Seasick Steve, he has not made many political statements, and superficial assessments of his whiskery, conservative appearance, and choice to appear on *Top Gear*, might lead to casual assumptions about his political leanings. Hearing poet Allen Cohen of the *San Francisco Oracle* talk about the movement's desire to challenge the establishment's greed and self-interest (there are several clips available on YouTube), for example, resonates with several comments Steve has made, and reminds us that he is, at heart, a hippie.

Steve has strong opinions about avarice and the profit

motive. In December 2008, as part of a Q&A for *The Guardian*, he answered 'greed' in response to the question 'What is the trait you most deplore in others?' Talking to Rick Levin of *The Stranger* in 2000 about his reasons for leaving Olympia and moving to Norway, he explained: 'I'm finished with America. I'm fifty years old now, and I've been watching greed play the main stage since I was a teenager. I just can't stand it any more.' In this respect, he is very much a son of Haight-Ashbury.

Glimpses of that sceptical attitude towards the business end of show business still emerge from time to time. Asked by Gemma Brosnan of *Unshredded* magazine in October 2010 about talent programmes such as *The X-Factor* and *America's Got Talent*, he condemned their cynical exploitation of talent and naïveté:

> Even if you win, nothing happens, somebody is working as a waitress or something and sprung into huge fame and it lasts about six months, it's a powerful drug for any young person and then within six months they are back working as a waitress. I don't like it man, not even for America or here . . . in general, it's just a money machine and I really hate it. I thought that the normal radio couldn't get any worse, but it did. Normal radio has been pretty bad since the Fifties with all this shit and then they figured out something else.

There are smaller cultural legacies as well that may have left their mark on him. Haight-Ashbury was where the rock poster as artwork was invented – initially and most famously by San Francisco band the Charlatans, but subsequently taken up by many others. As Steve created the collage of icons for his homemade sleeve for his album *Cheap* – with its classic American-hobo iconography of a train, a worn boot, a can of pork and beans, a loaf of Wonder bread and a label from a can of Sterno fuel gel (for camp cooking) – there's a tantalising sense that he may have had memories of the beautifully designed and crafted posters that would have been created all around him in Haight-Ashbury.

Steve seems to have been immune to appeal of the vibrant, swirling visual effects that accompanied many a rock gig at the time, however. Artist Bill Ham developed the first psychedelic liquid projection light shows that appeared at the Red Dog Saloon, and later the Avalon Ballroom. They don't seem to have left much impression on Steve, however. As you'd expect from a musician so dedicated to the analogue and authentic, he prefers to play without visual effects. Even smoke. 'Every time we play and there is a smoke machine, I'm like "Turn that f**king thing off" because it bothers me and nobody needs to see smoke pouring out behind us, so something's gone wrong,' he told *Unshredded* Magazine's Gemma Brosnan.

The pinnacle of Haight-Ashbury was, of course, the Summer of Love, and from a musical point of view, its highlight was the Monterey Pop Festival, held on 16–18 June in Monterey, on the coast just over a hundred miles south of San Francisco. Steve tells us in the *Telen* article of 13 November 2000 that he hitchhiked there. The event was held in the Monterey County Fairgrounds, previously the venue of the Monterey Jazz Festival, and the organisers were hoping to demonstrate that rock music could be marketed and performed as a serious art form. In this, they succeeded beyond their wildest dreams, as, according to some reports, up to 200,000 people attended the weekend overall. It became the template for other famous early rock festivals at Woodstock, in upstate New York, and the Isle of Wight in the UK, to name but two. Once again, Steve found himself in the front row of musical history, more or less by accident.

The line-up looks sensational with hindsight, but at the time, many of the acts had yet to break through, and were, like the concept for the event itself, a bit of a gamble. This was partly due to innumerable problems with the original list. Several acts declined their invitation, while other artists – Mick Jagger and Keith Richards of the Rolling Stones, for example – couldn't come because of immigration problems with drug convictions.

Some of the bands performing – Joplin, the Doors, the Grateful Dead and possibly also Jimi Hendrix – were already familiar to Steve from Haight-Ashbury, while others would have been tantalisingly new. Did Steve see Ravi Shankar or the South African jazz trumpeter Hugh Masekela? In the light of what we know about Steve's later involvement with Indian music, it's possible that this was the beginning of an important interest. That's less true in Masekela's case, but, even so, it does emphasise again how rich – especially for someone without any formal training – Steve's musical education and experience was.

The one act he mentions seeing by name (in *Telen*) is Jimi Hendrix, whose famously incendiary performance at Monterey was introduced by Brian Jones of the Rolling Stones. Hendrix had an address in Haight-Ashbury, but had been touring a lot, and it's possible Steve hadn't seen him perform before this gig. He has never claimed to know him as he did Joplin, however.

The Monterey set lists are a valuable reminder of how dependent 1960s rock was on the blues. Janis Joplin's greatest breakthrough piece was, of course, 'Ball and Chain', originally by the powerful feminist blues/soul singer Big Mama Thornton – who had an unfortunate habit of recording great songs such as this (which she also wrote) and a certain 'Hound Dog', only for white singers to cover them more successfully. Hendrix's set is another great example, and in that sense, as well as for the virtuosity of his playing, he must count as a big influence on Steve. His set included covers of BB King's 'Rock Me Baby', Howlin' Wolf's 'Killing Floor' and Bob Dylan's 'Like a Rolling Stone', as well as four originals – 'Foxy Lady', 'Can You See Me', 'The Wind Cries Mary' and 'Purple Haze'. Two of the most exciting and transformative features of this moment in music are the way in which black identities merged with white, and blues with rock, and soul. Although he's not always open about it himself, Steve embodies this fluidity of identity, and the depth and range of his musical experience is one of the key sources of his musical genius. Such important first-hand experience of so much blindingly original playing, and clues, from Hendrix and Joplin above all, of how the art and tradition of the blues could be forged into the powerful, modern style of rock, both on guitar and vocals, must linger long in Steve's memory.

Of the other features of Monterey's cultural legacy, one that – on the face of it, anyway – had less impact on Steve, is the development in the range and theatrical self-awareness of the performers' dress sense. Flamboyant, psychedelic hippie attire, with some thrift-store improvisation thrown in, had been a part of the Haight-Ashbury scene all along, but Monterey gave pop performers the first big platform to dress for a wider audience, and use their clothing to shape their public identity. Many performers embraced the challenge. Janis Joplin had become notorious for the raggedy, bohemian randomness of her attire, which initially became, for her many critics, a stick to beat her with. At Monterey, her performance of 'Ball and Chain' in particular was so sensational that people stopped talking about her appearance. But her fashion sense was always an important part of her originality, if not quite as strategically prepared as the best Monterey dresser.

And that, again, was Hendrix, the most successful example of image-shaping. Wearing what looks like an orange crêpe shirt with a ruff, a ribbon in his hair, a silk waistcoat designed by Chris Jagger – Mick's brother – and skin-tight nylon trousers, with his hair – apparently – curled to look like Bob Dylan's, Hendrix created a look that was not only unique, romantic, and original, but, perhaps more historically, managed to define himself independently from the racial stereotypes previously applied to African American performers. As Keith Shadwick, in his book *Jimi*

Hendrix: Musician notes, 'Hendrix was dressed in clothes as exotic as any on display elsewhere . . . He was not only something utterly new musically, but an entirely original vision of what a black American entertainer should and could look like.'

Hendrix's last touch of visual genius, of course, was to burn his guitar. Once the fire had taken hold, Hendrix kneeled behind it, coaxing the flames higher and higher with a mischievous grin. The photo taken of him at that moment became an iconic image of the festival, but it also says something bigger about what had happened in San Francisco – the combination of extreme violence and creativity, and the outrageous originality of both his playing and his persona. Hendrix commented that he burned the guitar as a sacrifice of something he loved, but there's so much more in that picture: it symbolises the irrepressible, yet self-destructive, charisma of Hendrix's own career, and, more broadly, the rapid rise of pop as a potent, yet in some ways evanescent and disposable, cultural force.

Looking at Steve now, we might think that Hendrix's blouse-like shirts and bell-bottoms were a different scene completely. Until the rerelease of the album *Shanti*, there were no publicly available photos of Steve before the mid-1990s. In the rehearsal shot in the album booklet, he's less flamboyant than Hendrix, in tight jeans and a vest top, but it's modern clothing, with no hint of the railroad about it. In the Shanti performance, however, which is now available on YouTube (by searching 'Shanti band'), Steve shows that he can dress for the hippie music scene as well as anyone, his lurid green-and-pink floral shirt and tight fawn trousers perhaps not quite in Hendrix's league still, but still vividly in keeping with the symbolism of the music.

As a recording engineer in the 1990s until about 2002, Steve presents, in photos, a relaxed, scruffy man in baggy jeans and sweatshirt, his beard generous and sprawling, like a nature reserve for rare species, and his bald head gleaming. When he starts performing as Seasick Steve (with the Level Devils), this becomes smarter, but dated, with indigo jeans and white T-shirt, to be followed, when the full Seasick identity is developed, by the flannel shirts, dungarees and John Deere caps we know today. He does clearly understand how to create a clear visual identity with his outfits: Seasick Steve is one of the most readily identifiable acts around. Monterey, especially Hendrix and Joplin, would have shown him how to create a strong visual identity.

Even after Steve had left home and was living right in the heart of San Francisco's burgeoning rock community, he remained active in the blues scene. This was partly because the two genres were much more closely connected then than they are now. It was because many blues artists were working on a smaller budget than the rock stars could command by the late sixties. And it must also have been because Steve grew up with the music and loved it (despite the denials we saw in the previous chapter), as we can see in his music today.

What is clear is that, until the creation of Seasick Steve and the alternate narrative of his early life, he was proud of having worked with – or even just seen – so many famous musicians. He revelled in their company, and this is an important part of what made him a brilliant musician. This comes across in what he tells Norway's *Telen* newspaper about his time in Haight-Ashbury. Likewise, in September 2002, he revealed Norwegian national newspaper *Dagbladet* that he had played with 'Joni Mitchell, the Beach Boys and the Grateful Dead'.

The clearest evidence for Steve's obvious pride in his musical past comes in an interview published by the webzine *Ear Pollution*, with one of his favourite bands, the Tremens, whom he recorded at his studio in Notodden. As well as providing an initial lead on Steve's involvement with Shanti, it mentions the Beach Boys and other sixties luminaries: 'Steve knows all those people . . . he knows everybody. And he's got stories you wouldn't believe. Everything from hitchhiking and getting picked up by Jimi Hendrix, to playing with people like Albert King and a ton of other blues guys. But the coolest thing about him is his attitude, which is simply "God forgive the soul who wants to be a rock star."'

We already know that Steve hitchhiked to Monterey – how exciting would it have been for both if it was Hendrix who had given him a lift?

There are two crucial things we learn from this quote. There's the obvious excitement Steve feels in sharing the details of his musical past – this is surely the real Steve, not the man we see today who restricts himself to talking about his blue-collar jobs and denies his musical past. And, of course, many of the star players he met, Joplin and Hendrix in particular, also provided case studies of the dangers of stardom. And the ambivalent attitude to his own past that we see in Seasick Steve today is surely influenced by this: one interpretation of the curious past that is 'Seasick' Steve is that, in creating a past that's to a large degree a smokescreen from what really happened, he's protecting himself and his family. It's simply a shame that until now his fascinating musical background has been obscured.

Other acts he claims to have performed with come up in his March 2006 interview with bluesinlondon.com: 'In the '60s he began to play at clubs on the West Coast and supported Son House amongst others. He played with Lightnin' Hopkins for a while and Freddie King too.' Joni Mitchell frequently appears in interviews, too. A March 2015 piece for *Discussions* magazine observes: 'He was playing live and in the studio with blues musicians in the Sixties, and has befriended and/or worked with artists as varied as Joni Mitchell and Modest Mouse.'

The California bands, including the Grateful Dead and the Beach Boys, Steve could have met and gigged with any time – especially the Beach Boys, because of the TM connection. It's also possible that he played with Son House, by this time one of the most important of the Delta bluesmen, but that can't be verified. House was living in Rochester, New York, by this time, right over the far side of the country from California. He was touring in the area in the mid- and late 1960s – for example, he opened the third annual UCLA Folk Festival in 1965 – but he usually played solo, and there are no records of his ever playing with Steve. I consulted Daniel Beaumont, author of Son House's biography, *Preachin' The Blues*, who observed,

Sometimes when Son House performed locally in Rochester after his rediscovery, he was backed by Joe Beard, or John Mooney and Brian Williams. But as far as I know, when Dick Waterman [Son House's booking agent] had him tour nationally or in Europe (mostly England, but he played Montreux at least once) he performed alone.

On the other hand, in Mississippi by the late thirties and early forties, he was always accompanied by Willie Brown. An occasional drummer, fiddle player, even a trombone sometimes. When Alan Lomax said he wanted to record him in 1941, Son's reply was something like, 'Let me get my boys . . .'

It seems unlikely that Steve could have become one of Son House's 'boys' midway through a tour, with no prior acquaintance. There is no hard evidence for it, anyway. So, when bluesinlondon.com says 'supported', it presumably means Steve played a set before those artists, on the same bill, rather than playing alongside them. Beaumont records an occasion in his biography when House was playing a gig at the Gaslight Café in Greenwich Village in 1965, and 'was on the bill with a young white singer-songwriter named Tom Paxton'. However, 'young' meant twenty-eight, not a teenager, as Steve would have been until he left for Paris, more or less. It would have been impossible for Steve to perform either with or alongside Son House.

I also asked Dick Waterman, who knew nothing of a young Steve Leach performing at one of House's gigs. He did tell me a cute story that took place in London, in 1969, though, which illustrates how permeable the blues scene was, and how a chance meeting might have come about:

> Son and I were walking down Portobello with a bright sun over our heads. This guitarist was sitting on the ground and we were sun blinded when he looked up. I asked him if he knew of Son House and he said that he was trying to raise money for a ticket. He could only see Son in silhouette because of the sun. So I asked him to stand up and he did and then realised that it was Son. I remember that we went to a pub and I bought him a sandwich and a beer and put his name on the backstage list.

There's no way that Steve was in London in 1969. But what this does show is that, even after rock became glamorous and commercialised, the blues scene worked on a smaller scale, and in a less formal manner. While it didn't work out for Steve with Son House, it did with Lightnin' Hopkins, as we shall see in a moment.

Before that, however, we also have to rule out Steve's working in any formal way with Joni Mitchell. Both she and Steve were active in California, so some kind of informal jam – or perhaps a bit of engineering work – is possible. Mitchell has unfortunately been too ill to approach, recently. Without being disrespectful to Steve, however, whose musical and production ability should never be underestimated, Mitchell's recording career was taking off rapidly in the late sixties, when she might have met him. She had a settled professional recording setup, and it's not clear what she would have done with an obscure, if talented, teenage blues guitarist.

The only specific information connecting Steve and Joni Mitchell was published in the *San Diego Tribune*, in an article entitled 'Seasick Steve grounded in the blues', on 6 February 2014: 'He went on to play with John Lee Hooker and do pre-production work on Joni Mitchell's *Court and Spark* album.' That Mitchell album – her most successful – wasn't released until 1974, and was recorded during much of the previous year. Yet, even by 1973, Steve was – by his own admission – busking in the Paris Metro. There's no record of his name in any of the album's documentation and the writer doesn't say where the story came from, but the piece is a glowing preview of a show Steve was giving, so there would presumably have been some collaboration with Steve's staff or PR. As for John Lee Hooker and Freddie King, Hooker seems more likely to have worked with Steve – and he's a more interesting prospect in this sense, in terms of the similarity of their playing styles. Freddie King was touring (sometimes overseas) and recording almost constantly during the late sixties – his exhausting schedule was one of the causes of his early death soon afterwards – and he wasn't based in California.

Hooker, on the other hand, moved to Oakland, California, in about 1970, and spent much of the decade in various collaborations with, among others, Canned Heat and Van Morrison. It's entirely possible, but not certain, that Hooker could have used a talented young guitarist and recording engineer for some of this work in 1970–2, especially if he had been recommended by

Lightnin' Hopkins. Hooker and Hopkins, then, are not only the most likely to have played with Steve at this time (in Hopkins's case it's certain) but are the most important stylistic influences. It may be even simpler than that: if Steve did play with Hooker and Hopkins about this time, when he was eighteen or twenty, and his mature guitar style was still forming, it's likely to be their influence, to some extent, that we hear coming through.

Perhaps the best commentary on Steve's musical style comes from his profile on the website thecountryblues. com, which states,

> Seasick Steve, Richard Johnston, Ben Prestage etc. learned much from the Mississippi Hill Country masters, the famous forefathers Junior Kimbrough and RL Burnside. Seasick, Prestage and Johnston like to play the three-string diddley bow type cigar box guitars. Seasick even strips his guitars down to three strings. Junior Kimbrough and RL Burnside got down with a strange juke joint brew, a magical amalgam of some of the funky boogie of John Lee Hooker, a dash of Lightning [sic] Hopkins and a couple of spoons of plain out soul and funk. Both John Lee and Lightning Hopkins could sit solo, all by themselves, and get down to a funky boogie that had everyone in the house shake their booty, because they fully understood the importance of a beat.

Both players, then, could command a stage and move an audience using the power of rhythm. In Hooker's case especially, there sometimes wasn't much else going on from a musical point of view – he wasn't an especially technical player – but his grasp of mood and atmosphere was sensational. Like Steve, Hooker has a dark, mesmerising voice (perhaps rather spookier than Steve's), a driving, rhythmic style with roots in boogie, and he tended to stomp along to his guitar. Listen to Steve's songs that owe most to the Hooker influence ('Seasick Boogie' and 'Hobo Low', say) alongside any of Hooker's famous tracks ('Boom Boom', for example, or 'Boogie Chillen'), and the echoes are unmistakable.

Hooker encapsulates the development of the blues during the twentieth century in a single career, more than anyone else. Born in 1917 in Clarksdale, Mississippi, to a sharecropping family, he grew up in the centre, both historically and geographically, of the development of the Delta blues and must often have seen Charlie Patton and Son House during his youth in 1920s. At the same time, his own style of powerful modal vamps and propulsive, mesmeric rhythm derive not so much from the Delta style, which used slide guitar and rhythmic variation, but from the influence of Louisiana's primal funk, as taught to the young Hooker by Will Moore, his stepfather from Shreveport. Moore was a popular guitarist in the Delta of the 1920s, often playing with Patton and House, among others, but his sound and technique were very different.

It's believed that the Louisiana blues – exemplified by Robert Pete Williams – is more closely related to the African traditional music slaves brought with them than the Delta blues, which was suppressed by nervous landowners frightened of its potential to provoke an uprising. (Louisiana landowners were repressive too, but less afraid of revolt.) The rolling, trancelike beat heard in Hooker is quite simple, technically, but requires a high degree of performing charisma – as we also find in Steve's rhythmically mesmeric tracks. Is Steve's potent and unmistakeable guitar beat a direct throwback to a ceremonial style brought directly from West Africa?

Hopkins was originally from Texas, where a chance encounter with Blind Lemon Jefferson at the age of eight gave him a wonderful introduction to the music business. The two worked together for many years. He was more sophisticated technically than Hooker, and sounds, most of the time, a bit more like Steve. His guitar was tuned low to accommodate his gravelly, drawling voice (another similarity between the two), and his dark glasses asserted a cool persona that's different from Steve's stage presence, but similarly powerful.

Hopkins exploited a finger-picking, rhythmically complex guitar style, in which sometimes the guitar and his own singing were in syncopation, creating a very different kind of atmosphere from Hooker, though one that's more subtly engrossing. He's generally more mellow than Steve, and the subject matter is usually more conventional, but there are moments when Steve picks rather than thumps like Hooker, when his balance of gently swinging voice and guitar, is very similar. Just listen to 'Shirly Lou', 'Whiskey Ballad' or 'Treasures'.

Hooker and Hopkins enjoyed a similar career path. After initial success in the 1940s, the meagre returns offered by record companies then left them scratching an irregular touring income in the 1950s, until the 1960s brought a new and better-paying audience – college students yearning for an 'authentic' folk-blues sound. Both musicians experimented with rock collaborations later on, and some of Hooker's have lasted reasonably well, including the recordings with rockers Canned Heat that he set down sooner after he moved to California, and on which Steve may have lent a hand. In this respect, however, Steve has accomplished something neither of his (possible) mentors ever really mastered: in his career as a backing player and engineer, and since coming to fame as Seasick Steve and playing with the likes of John Paul Jones, Steve has shown that he can rock with the best of them. When they tried, Hooker and Hopkins were both known to befuddle rockers with an approach to timing that had a bit too much country blues about it.

We can be pretty certain where and when Steve played with Lightnin' Hopkins: on a West Coast tour (sponsored by a chain of pizza parlours), probably in 1969. Unusually for a musical commitment at this point in his life, Steve has mentioned the occasion, albeit obliquely. Steve was giving a Q&A to *The Guardian* in December 2008, and in response to a question about his most embarrassing moment, said, 'Forty years ago in Seattle I tried to tell Lightnin' Hopkins that he wasn't changing chords at the right place in a blues song.' Forty years ago in 2008 is 1968, of course, so an approximate match chronologically, and Seattle would be a good fit with the West Coast destinations. It's a cute little vignette: Steve was only eighteen at the time but had just had four years in the musical crucible of Haight-Ashbury and had clearly become a confident guitarist.

There are other clues. In 2011, talking to Thomas H Green of *The Arts Desk*, and responding to a question about Led Zeppelin, Steve commented, 'I saw them play in 1969. I was playing at a pizza parlour and this guy came in and asked if I wanted to see an English blues band. We went over to this amphitheatre and saw them play. Man, they was good.'

The Hopkins tour is the only such tour with any authentication. The only places where Led Zeppelin appeared that could be described as an amphitheatre are the San Diego Sports Arena (played on 10 August 1969) and the Fairgrounds Arena (now called the Earl Warren Showgrounds, which they played on 1 August 1969) in Santa Barbara, which fits with the West Coast itinerary. It would be interesting if we could place Steve for certain in Santa Barbara, because he came back to live there in 1977 with his first wife Victoria and two baby sons. But we can't be sure.

There's one last name worth mentioning. In October 2008, Steve told *The Scotsman*: 'I could have played with Mississippi Fred McDowell and I didn't do it, because I had other important things to do, I don't know what it was. Now I'm just grateful that I got to see them [the previous generation of bluesmen] and play a little bit.'

McDowell died in 1972, so Steve must be referring here to his San Francisco years. Unlike the other bluesmen Steve performed alongside, McDowell lived in Mississippi, and the fact the opportunity arose (if it did) shows how much

Steve was on the radar of older black bluesmen needing competent support. McDowell was not from the Delta but Como, in the north of the state, not far from Memphis, Tennessee. (This is, probably coincidentally, where Steve's friend Sherman lives, who bought the $25, allegedly haunted, guitar later to become the Three-String Trance Wonder.)

The blues from that region is – a little like Louisiana's, as we saw in the case of Shreveport-born Will Moore, who taught the young John Lee Hooker – supposedly closer to the structure of the original African music brought with the first generation of slaves. Instead of the characteristic Delta blues chord change, Hill Country blues uses a single-chord vamp, for a haunting, hypnotic effect. As we saw in the case of Hooker and his influence on Steve, this is an effect that can sometimes be detected in some of Steve's bleaker songs

There's one last reason why it made sense for him to stay around San Francisco. In March 2006, Steve told bluesinlondon.com, 'I'd learnt how to do music engineering in the late sixties, being a technician or coffee maker or whatever in a studio, so could fall back on that kind of a job. I started buying pieces of equipment so I could build my own studio some day.' Steve comes back to the experience of learning the art of recording on analogue equipment when talking to the Norwegian newspaper *Dagbladet* in August 2001 about the opening of his studio, renamed Juke Joint, in Notodden:

It's not just Wold who is gripped by retro wave. Many musicians dream of making records in a vintage studio. 'For many years, no one bothered to give these wonderful studios a second thought. Many ended up in the rubbish dump when everything was about to be digitised. But it was this equipment I learned working in the studio on, so I had not the heart. And anyway, it is the musicians' qualities and the quality of the songs, which determines whether it is a good disc,' concludes Steve Wold.

One feature of Steve's attitudes and psychological development we must allow for is that, without any emotional support from family, he seems to have invested much more in other formative experiences. One explanation that has presented itself for the extraordinary lengths he has gone to to deflect attention from what he was really doing in these years is that both the practice of music and the community of people he spent time with over this period mean much more to him – to the point, in some respects, of being surrogate family – than similar experiences would to most other people. He has spent most of his professional life running, or being involved with, music studios. That analogue recording equipment he couldn't bear to throw away became his much-loved personal history, not just a job.

Clearly, he didn't learn music engineering on a train in Mississippi, and studio work being (like guitar-playing) a sporadic and often unpredictable kind of employment, he would have needed to be on hand much of the time if he wanted to gain any substantial engineering time. It's also worth reminding ourselves how important the idea of owning a studio was to Steve, and how early it took root. All the more traumatic, then, when the studio he'd built up since the early 1990s in Olympia failed in Norway, and he lost most of his equipment, sold for a pittance. That sort of bad luck would make anyone turn in on themselves to some extent.

The piecing together of this period of Steve's life would always be complicated while Steve himself insists he was riding trains. It's all too likely that the vagueness of some of the stories in the period 1967–70 reflects the reality of Steve's life: he was still a teenager, learning to be a professional musician, and with no money, family or contacts behind him. His musical engagements were probably irregular, and spread among many different genres from Lightnin' Hopkins, via the Beach Boys and Grateful Dead, to the Indian fusion band Shanti that was his big, professional breakthrough, and his first (we assume) recording credit. The details of Shanti's recording and live performances suggest a very serious professional undertaking, which producer Richard Bock was expecting to be very successful. Musically, Steve had arrived – which must have made it frustrating when he departed again a couple of years later.

According to Richie Unterberger's album notes, Shanti had formed officially 'around late 1970' (October that year, according to *Rolling Stone*). But, as we've seen, the four American players were already well acquainted from what sounds like at least a year's meditation together. Steve was one of three players recruited for his pop experience, according to guitarist Neil Seidel: 'There were several components to Shanti. There was the rock'n'roll component, the pop component, which was in the form of Francisco [drummer Frank Lupica], Steve Leach, and Steve Haehl. Those three players were pretty much strictly pop musicians.' This is interesting, insofar as it gives us an idea how Steve was perceived by his contemporaries. By the sound of it, he was better known for his work with the Beach Boys than with the bluesmen.

Once the band's line-up was established, producer Richard Bock and manager Michael Davenport furnished the American players with a house in San Anselmo, Marin County, about twenty miles north of San Francisco. As Neil Seidel recalls, 'Basically, we got our rent paid and he bought us some instruments, which we were able to use. We got like about $35 a week spending money.' Assuming Steve stayed there (wives are not mentioned) until the band folded in 1972, that's two years of his early life when we know he was living in a settled way near San Francisco – something Steve's British fans, at least, have never before known.

According to Unterberger, 'Shanti recorded their sole album in September 1971 at one of San Francisco's top studios, Pacific High Recording, with Bock in the producer's seat.' The sound we can hear on the album today is apparently faithful to the band's live sound, recalls Seidel: 'I thought it was very indicative of what we sounded like. We didn't sound any different onstage than we did in the studio.' Shanti's live gigs – even their rehearsal conditions – confirm how well integrated Steve and Shanti were to the rock scene. They used to rehearse, says, Unterberger 'at Grateful Dead drummer Mickey Hart's in the Marin

County town of Novato', which was also the location for a live broadcast 'that featured Jerry Garcia and the New Riders of the Purple Sage'.

One of the benefits of Shanti's eclectic (and, at that time, pretty original) style was that they could be paired with a wide range of other acts. And there was plenty of quality around at the time to choose from. Neil Seidel recalls: 'We played at the Fillmore with Humble Pie and Swamp Dogg. We played at the Ash Grove in Los Angeles with Commander Cody and His Lost Planet Airmen. We played with Ali Akbar Khan in San Francisco' – the last a reference to a gig at the Palace of Fine Arts. They were also matched with Little Feat in Berkeley, and Joan Baez at the Hollywood Bowl. 'So they would put us with anybody. We could interface with any music mix,' says Seidel.

The album *Shanti* contains seven tracks that span in character the full breadth of the band's generic range. 'Innocence' and 'Shanti', by far the longest, are instrumental pieces composed by Khan to show the character and potential of the Indian instruments. The rest, all under four minutes long, have lyrics, a much poppier sensibility, and the compositions try to blend the Indian and Western instruments. The opening track, 'We Want To Be Free', is perhaps the most successful demonstration of where the band could have struck gold, if given a bit longer. The structure of the piece is straight pop, but the tones and colour of the Indian instruments, especially Khan's sarod, come through strongly and charismatically. 'Out of Nowhere' and 'I Do Believe' use a freer, arguably more traditionally Indian structure, and as such are possibly more original, though most modern listeners will find the blandly religiose lyrics rather tiresome.

Circus (a popular American rock magazine that ran from 1966 to 2006) declared the album 'one of the most organic meldings of Eastern music and rock and roll ever recorded', although in 1971 there wasn't a great deal of competition. From the vantage point of 2015, the quality of the playing comes through clearly, but there is probably too much stylistic diversity for one record. It's easy to imagine a label's marketing department having reservations about the lack of audience focus. It must be said, through all of this, that Steve's contributions, both on bass and to the vocals, are easy to miss. Fans listening out for a bit of slide guitar, or that unmistakable molasses baritone, will be disappointed.

Although *Shanti* received good reviews at the time, and there are plenty of glowing assessments online today – on the band's YouTube page, for example – they were, perhaps, a bit too difficult to categorise to be easily sold. On the one hand, they were doing something serious and idealistic, but, on the other, they were pop rather than art music, as jazz guitarist John McLaughlin's bands the Mahavishnu Orchestra and Shakti were. Khan and Hussain have gone on to very successful careers in Indian music, and there are some reports that Ravi Shankar (the Indian classical musician who had played an important role in popularising Indian classical music in the West, and collaborated many times with Beatles guitarist George Harrison) feared that the pair would lose this skill if they were to become swallowed up by the pop scene too early.

Hussain, speaking on the *Jake Feinberg Show* in 2012, said that Shankar 'wanted Aashish Khan and I to realise that we have this incredible gift that has been given to us by our forefathers, and we should not mess with it in a way where it loses its identity'.

According to some versions of the band's demise, there were prospects that George Harrison was interested in signing Shanti for Apple Records after the Atlantic contract had finished, but that Ravi Shankar advised him not to for the same reason. Neil Seidel believes, meanwhile, that Atlantic Records' apathy was substantially to blame for the band's failure: 'Atlantic did nothing for us. Zero . . . There was no interest in us [from Atlantic], really.'

Shanti carried on performing well into 1972, but once the prospect of a new recording contract was definitely past, it seems to have folded quite quickly. Zakir Hussain went on to collaborate with John McLaughlin's fusion projects, and has become a well-known advocate of East–West musical fusion; Aashish Khan had a successful career as an Indian classical musician; and Neil Seidel went on to become a film-music composer. Steve has arguably had a career as successful and distinctive as any, though it is peculiar and unfortunate that he has done so while disowning not just Shanti, but his whole past as Steve Leach. His fans would surely have greater insight into the originality of his current act if they knew the musical richness he has learned from along the way.

Our knowledge of Steve's involvement in Shanti, and the prior commitment to the Transcendental Meditation it entails, rules out definitively his having any period of homelessness lasting longer than a few months. That period, if it happened at all, must surely have taken place in California, not Mississippi. It's an impressive achievement for Steve to have made it into a professional band operating on this sort of level, giving private gigs to George Harrison and Ravi Shankar, and sharing a stage with some of the best acts of the day, especially as he left home five years earlier being able to play only a few chords, and apparently being more proficient on the trombone. To have achieved what he did, however, must have required constant practice, and lots of networking – not something he could have achieved unless he remained in the Bay Area throughout. The extra decade shoehorned into the official Seasick Steve biography before he arrived at Haight-Ashbury feels like an admission that there wasn't enough time afterwards to gain authentic hobo credentials. Readers must come to their own conclusions.

If we put the hobo lifestyle to one side as largely myth, we can also discount another of Steve's colourful stories. Being a hobo always carried the risk of being arrested, and Steve has often told of his regular penitentiary visits. As *The Scotsman* noted in October 2008:

> He won't confirm his age, only adding to the mystique of a fascinating life which encompasses such verifiable facts and figures as five kids, two wives, 59 houses, countless jobs, and even a spell in jail. 'A spell?' he chuckles. 'I had plenty of spells . . . I wouldn't be wanting to put the counter on that.'

The offences that a young hobo such as Steve might have committed, and that would have led to imprisonment in the late sixties, would have included public intoxication, loitering, aggressive panhandling and vagrancy. Misdemeanours such as these are handled differently from state to state, and even district to district. Vagrancy was seldom prosecuted on its own, and if Steve was travelling from job to job – fruit picking, working on funfairs and the like – then neither aggressive panhandling nor vagrancy would have applied. So, unless we are to believe that young Steve was a particularly aggressive and incontinent drunk, or was involved in fighting, or theft (which has never been suggested), it's hard to see why he would have been imprisoned.

Steve's first wife, Victoria, although she was his partner for almost exactly the decade of 1970s, has almost entirely been airbrushed from his accounts of this period of his life. Of course, that may partly be to protect her, though it seems that, given the other ways in which Steve has edited his biography, it's possibly to emphasise the solitary adventurousness of his existence at this time. Victoria Johnson did not want to discuss her relationship with Steve, but, according to their son Sevrin, it was, at least to begin with, a happy if turbulent one. Steve has more of a temper than he lets on.

There is a clue about their relationship from the YouTube video of Shanti's performance, in which Steve is wearing what is almost certainly a wedding ring. Given the religious and philosophical nature of the band, and the fact that by the time the video was made, in 1971 or

1972, he must have been involved with Transcendental Meditation for at least two years, it's reasonable to assume Victoria was also a meditator. It's likely that they met through the practice, and also probable (as we will see) that both Victoria and Steve's second wife Elisabeth were actively involved in TM.

We know that later on Steve and Victoria's lack of money became a significant source of friction, but without children, in the laid-back communal atmosphere of San Francisco, two young music lovers must have had a blissful time together – blissful enough, anyway, for them to move to France together for five years. As Steve told bluesinlondon. com: 'I left [California] in 1972, and moved to France. Everything had gone down the shitter and I didn't have nowhere to go and I saw this charter flight for $100 to Paris, and I had $110. So I landed over there with 10 bucks. I got to that Charles De Gaulle airport and a fella gave me a ride right to that Left Bank thing where all the people were and I just started playing outside on the street, doing the same thing I'd done years before.'

When he says 'I' he means 'we'. Otherwise, this tallies with everything else we know about Steve around this time. What does Steve mean by 'gone down the shitter'? Knowing, as we do, that an exciting band, with a spiritual connection for Steve, and a recording contract with a major label, had just broken up, this is probably what he's thinking about most of all. Had Atlantic released another Shanti album, and had the band had longer to establish itself with audiences, Steve could almost certainly have built a musical career in California. He'd probably still be there now. Would he have had as much fun, and would we have music as good, if he had?

His negative feelings about California may also have related to Janis Joplin's death. That must have hurt. Of the members of rock's tragic '27 Club', Steve was friends with Joplin, he saw Hendrix perform at Monterey and would have seen Jim Morrison with the Doors in San Francisco, too. He would later live near Kurt Cobain in Olympia (though they weren't friends, exactly), and performed alongside Amy Winehouse on Jools Holland's *Hootenanny*. His connectedness to this macabre offside to the music scene is remarkable. His own survival skills, meanwhile, are remarkably robust.

Joplin's loss would have been compounded by the collapse of the musical community – in some respects Steve's first real family, and certainly his best friends – within Haight-Ashbury, although it was probably replaced to some extent by the Transcendental Meditation community, and the players around Shanti. But, when both were gone, the gigging and engineering jobs and the associated social life were lost, too.

As the record industry understood how much money there was to be made in rock music, the whole business of recording and gigging rapidly professionalised. Studios expanded, and used a more regular roster of engineers and backing musicians. The loose, informal, creative community that had existed at Haight-Ashbury was being commercialised and formalised, and someone young and unknown, without strong contacts, was always going to struggle. The older forms of music, such as the blues, were still working on a smaller scale, in a less formal way. Someone young, cheap and relatively flexible such as Steve was perfect for Lightnin' Hopkins. In fact, he has preferred things to stay small-scale, local and low-key throughout his career – until, that is, the big time came to find him. As disappointments mounted in San Francisco towards the end of 1972, it's entirely understandable he and Victoria chose a Parisian romance for their next adventure.

CHAPTER 5

Paris and Children

In terms of his personal life, the next eight years of Steve's life were hugely important. Nothing really happened for him musically, though it wasn't for want of trying. But his family changed a lot. He gained two sons, then left his wife, and began the 1980s much as he'd began the 1970s – a wandering guitar for hire. The established facts about this period in Steve's life don't take long to explain, so we will then consider a little more the dynamics of his closest family relationships, with the help of some intriguing contributions from Steve's eldest son, Sevrin Johnson.

Sevrin was keen to talk when I first got in touch. Known as 'Rev Sev', he still lives in Washington State, in the town of Monroe, ninety miles northeast of Olympia, the far side of Seattle. He leads and writes the music for a pop-punk band called Peratus, who are active in the region, with a lively online fan base, and millions of YouTube likes. Over a series of evenings, we had a fascinating conversation online. He and his younger brother Ivan clearly have raw feelings still about what happened with their father and mother.

Sevrin describes his parents as 'both very passionate people', but their relationship as 'rough'. 'They had fun travelling around Europe,' he admits – 'that's why I was born in France.' But when they got back to the States in late 1977, with two young children to look after, the poverty seems to have overcome the fun of the musician's life, leading to a more and more confrontational relationship, until the marriage collapsed completely. In Sev's words, it was 'cool' but they were 'dead poor through all that time'. Steve and Victoria were, after all, still in their mid-twenties when their second child arrived, which is a lot of responsibility to handle when one half of the marriage has a burning and as-yet unfulfilled musical ambition. 'They were young, they made bad decisions. I remember lots of yelling,' Sev says.

We can start with the fun they had in Europe. Sev was born – presumably in Paris, where it would have been easiest for Steve to make a living busking, on 9 March 1975, so they had only a couple of years of really carefree living before they had to begin a more settled lifestyle. Steve has been mostly reticent about these years, but there are a few leads. His reply to a *Guardian* Q&A in February 2008 is a start: 'In the early 1970s. I'd been on the trains a long time, but I knew someone in Paris who asked me if I wanted to go there to busk. I flew there with $10 in my pocket. Life was pretty much the same as in the States: I played on the streets and slept in parks, but I liked France better.' We can, of course, discount the first part about the hobo life. Was, the friend Victoria, who is otherwise completely airbrushed from his life? We can also assume they had somewhere more homely than parks to sleep in by, at the latest, mid-1974, when Victoria was pregnant.

He elaborated a little to Thomas H Green of *The Arts Desk* in June 2011: 'I don't think I really knew where Europe was. I just got a charter ticket, $100 one way, and landed at Charles de Gaulle airport with $10. I just stood there with a bewildered look at the airport and somebody asked me, "What do you want to do?" "Play guitar." "Go play in front of cafés." They told me what they should've, to go to St Germain, and I played on the street. I slept in Luxembourg Park which closed at 6pm so I'd sneak in and sleep in the bushes by a gazebo, come out in the morning and start again. I'd been playing on the streets a long time before I figured out there was a metro. I didn't understand where everyone was going. I thought it was a toilet.'

San Francisco's Muni Metro network has had some underground sections since 1918, albeit on nothing like the scale of Paris. Did Steve really not understand where these Parisian metro passengers were going? More importantly, a variety of sources (including the Neuland Concerts 2009 press release, which is not always reliable but in this case there's no reason to suspect its accuracy) agree that most of Steve's money in these years was made busking on the Paris Metro.

Paris in 1972 was still settling down after the uprising of May 1968, in which a series of protests were eventually quelled by the autocratic and haughty President Charles de Gaulle. The uprising was started by students, but spread to factories and eventually led to a general strike and a series of violent street demonstrations. De Gaulle called new elections, which he won, but the protesters' point was made, and wide-ranging reforms were made to the structure of many of France's often bureaucratic and hierarchical institutions. The following year, De Gaulle resigned, leaving the more businesslike and pragmatic Georges Pompidou to take over. He embarked on a programme of economic modernisation up to his sudden death in 1974.

While Steve was there, France had recent experience of radical protest, in some ways more widespread and destabilising than the events in Haight-Ashbury. The country was also culturally and politically more confident and forward-looking than it had been for decades. One of Pompidou's first changes to the political setup De Gaulle had bequeathed was to improve relations with America. So to the existing French fondness for American roots music we can add an improving international relationship. Steve must have had a warm welcome.

Presumably, Steve was playing country blues to Parisian commuters, and must on the whole have been considered rather retro and quaint. Paris did not have a Haight-Ashbury, or a Summer of Love as such, but avant-garde rock of all kinds was in the air by the time Steve arrived, which would have contrasted markedly with his rustic guitar playing. It's still the case that the most popular French musicians known outside France are predominantly the *chansonniers*

Edith Piaf, George Brassens and Serge Gainsbourg; some, such as Charles Trenet, were still singing in that style until the 1990s. However, the Anglo-Saxon world is less familiar with the busy French left-field rock scene, which was quite active by the time Steve arrived.

Jean-Pierre Massiera invented French progressive rock with a series of sprawling, adventurous, multi-genre explorations that, despite his prodigious musical skill, still have only a cult following. His debut, *Les Maledictus Sound* (1968), is a sprawling melange of prog, psychedelia and jazz-funk, involving up to a dozen musicians. There were rock operas, such as Magma's *Mëkanïk Dëstruktïẁ Kömmandöh* (1973), and weird and wonderful concept albums. Red Noise released the baffling *Sarcelles-Locheres* (1971), a blend of free jazz and proto-noise taking in Frank Zappa and Soft Machine and adding the band's own curious satirical twist. And there were more large-scale instrumental suites from the likes of Vangelis and Jean-Claude Vannier, the latter the arranger of Serge Gainsbourg's lavish, funky *Histoire de Melody Nelson* (1971), a rather brilliant suite about a pervert and a nymphet. All of which is to say that the scene at which Steve arrived in 1972 was rapidly becoming one of the most bizarre and adventurous in Europe, and at least some of Steve's audience were musically sophisticated and cosmopolitan. It would be wonderful – albeit impossible – to know what Steve sounded like then and whether there was much Haight-Ashbury influence in his performances.

We can only assume, since he did it for five years, and latterly supported Victoria and baby Sevrin on what he

SEASICK STEVE

earned, that he made enough to live on. He's never said anything about learning the French language, and it's difficult to imagine him breaking into the heavily unionised world of the sort of blue-collar trades he did some of the time back home. Nor does he seem to have made contact with the French musical world to tour, back other musicians or play sessions. So he busked for five years, continuously apart from their various travel breaks. Perhaps the main conclusion to draw from this otherwise rather blank period in Steve's life is just how incredibly good he must have become at playing guitar. Four or five hours' practice most days, and in an environment where people tell you straight if they don't like what they hear, must be one of the secrets of his later success.

Steve tells some amusing tales about his time in Europe. Interviewed by Swiss channel SRF 3 in 2014, he told a story of living rough in a park in Paris in 1972, and, hearing that the American Embassy in Bern would send destitute Americans home for free, he travelled all the way to Bern, to try his luck. The ambassador, however, was having none of it, and sent Steve packing with a flea in his ear, so he walked into the town and began busking, earning only enough to buy a bag of roast chestnuts. His playing attracted some local teenage music fans, who took pity on Steve, put him up in what he says was their grandmother's flat, and arranged for him to give a concert at the local youth centre in a week's time. The gig raised $750, which was a lot in 1972, sufficient to keep Steve going for months. One of the Swiss fans took a photo of Steve with a God's Eye, the woven hippie sacred token, and Steve sent the photo home to his dad, Gene, who apparently had it on his wall at home in California when he died.

It's a lovely, touching tale, full of quirky human interest and strange coincidence – the sort Steve narrates well in his more expansive tracks – and is odd enough to be true. We can get a flavour of his travels with Victoria's from this story, told to Thomas H Green of *The Arts Desk*, which suggests that the community of American musicians travelling around Europe at the time was a warm and intriguing bunch. Green asks Steve, 'By the early fifties singers such as Woody Guthrie, Pete Seeger and Ramblin' Jack Elliott had very much associated American roots music with protest and even socialism. What did you think about that?' Steve replies,

> I like Rambling [*sic*] Jack. I met Derroll Adams wandering around Europe in the Seventies. He was one of the Almanac Singers who'd left America after the Korean War in protest. He said to me, 'When you get back to America and run into Rambling Jack give him a kiss on the cheek and a pinch on the butt from me.' I go, 'Derroll, America's a big place,' but sure enough I ran straight into Rambling Jack when I got back. I said, 'Jack, I'm supposed to give you a kiss on the cheek and a pinch on the butt from Derroll Adams but I'm not going to do it.' I never knew about that protest thing, not until the sixties, the only one I knew was the Almanac Singers singing 'The House of the Rising Sun'.

One answer, of course, is that Steve was far too young to take in what was happening to the folk scene in the fifties. But the more important point, in this context, is the impression given of the warm, humorous company of other musicians that Steve and Victoria met on the road. This must have been part of the 'great fun' Sevrin says they had in those years, and it must have broken up the routine of playing on the Paris metro very enjoyably.

After five years in France, they flew to the very different environment of Maui, Hawaii, where Steve's son Ivan was born on 7 July 1977; Paul Martin Wold, Steve's youngest son with Elisabeth, would be born on Kauai, Hawaii, in 1988. Steve and Victoria must have left France in June, at the latest. Once we've established that Steve was a committed follower of Transcendental Meditation, both of the Hawaii birthing visits make much more plausible sense, though the connection cannot be proven definitively. Although, of course, Hawaii is undoubtedly an agreeable and relaxing holiday destination, there must have been a stronger reason for them to visit to give birth there, especially this first time, when money was so tight.

There are TM centres on all of the islands of Hawaii. Meditation is believed to be especially helpful during pregnancy and childbirth, controlling blood pressure, stress and cholesterol, aiding sleep, and even suppressing the pain of labour itself. This book is not the place to debate whether these claims are actually true, but simply to report that a TM adherent such as Steve (and probably Victoria, too) may have been readily persuaded that it could help.

They didn't stick around there more than a few months,

however, presumably because the work wasn't there for Steve, and once Ivan was old enough to fly they left for the equally agreeable Californian city of Santa Barbara. Originally a Spanish colonial town, it has an attractive, Mediterranean atmosphere and is set on the lowers slopes of the Santa Ynez Mountains, with the Los Padres forest just behind.

One of the disputed issues about Steve's working life during the course of the next fifteen years, until he settled into Moon Music in the nineties, is how much time he spent working on music, and how much on the other work he did. There's no doubt he did spend time on heavy-duty, blue-collar work. Sevrin mentions carpentry and framing (constructing the timber roof frames in new houses) as something Steve spoke of doing at this time. Elsewhere Steve has mentioned all kinds of labouring or low-level sales jobs.

Although Steve has sometimes denied it, there was always music in the background too. In the Swiss SRF 3 interview dating from 2014, he claims to be able to count on the fingers of 'one or maybe two hands' the number of times he played the guitar while he was bringing up his kids. To be fair, he doesn't set dates on this, but his children with his second wife Elisabeth weren't grown up until long after they moved to Norway in 2001. Yet he has recording credits with some of the bands he engineered in his studio in Olympia in the nineties. Is he not including those? It's all rather vague.

In fact, it seems likely he was actively pursuing a professional music career from the moment the family returned to the USA. The Neuland Concerts press release from November 2009 – an official document from Steve's record company, after all – presents itself as 'the facts, so far as he remembers them' (though there are the usual moments of convenient amnesia about his age), It states,

> For most of the 1970s Steve supported himself, his first wife and their two boys, working at whatever blue collar jobs he could find. 'I tried anything.' He recalls spending some time in Europe, busking in the Paris metro, before returning to America where he skittered around living in motels, cars, and when funds permitted, rented accommodation. The best it ever got was the music gigs, when he was hired as a studio engineer or played guitar in scratch bands for stars he would rather not mention 'because I hate name dropping, and anyways, they was just jobs'.

So he was, then, gigging and engineering all along, and, within the family, open about whom he was performing alongside. This fits in with several things Sevrin has said about his recollection of Steve as father. Firstly, it does seem clear that music was still Steve's priority:

> Ya, I was always aware of the famous people he worked with, music was definitely first and foremost for him, at my mother's, brother's and my expense. But he was young . . . a problem I understand better at my age now. I remember

almost everything growing up with him, when he was around, because I idolised him.

When I asked whether Steve was an affectionate father, interested in his children, Sevrin replied,

[He was] very all those things with my youngest three brothers from his second marriage, but with Ivan and me [he was] hardly ever around. When he was around, I remember it mostly being fun, him teaching me to surf, hanging out on the beach for a week or a weekend, then he was gone again. He would send us tapes of music and him talking to us. I loved that.

Sevrin is, clearly, upset about some aspects of his childhood, and that has motivated his commentary to some extent. But his account tallies almost completely with what the Neuland Concerts press release says about Steve's gigs, and travelling. A picture emerges of a young, ambitious man, determined to make it in music. He seems to have had a real knack for engaging fatherhood – what better way to communicate with your young sons if you're away on a recording project than send some tapes of your voice, and the music, back to your young sons? His human warmth is obvious from his musical performances. But the music still came first, and clearly that stung Sevrin.

Although no names are mentioned in the Neuland Concerts release, Sevrin recalls some of the bands Steve was working with: 'Yes, he would tell us about who he was working with. I was proud and saw him play an impromptu show with Slash [a.k.a. Saul Hudson, lead guitarist] from Guns N' Roses, and Seymour Duncan's band the Star Cowboys once.' Given that Sevrin was only two when they arrived in Santa Barbara, and Guns N' Roses released their debut album in 1987, this would have been during the late eighties. But it does show that Steve was working at a fairly high level, with important names. It was reasonable for him to think that he'd make it – which, of course, eventually, he did.

It was a stressful lifestyle for the whole family, who were 'dead poor through all that time', Sevrin recalls. That must have been difficult for Victoria, left alone with two young sons and very little cash. The strains of the situation – emotional, financial, professional – were evident even to young Sevrin: 'But, as loving as he was, he was also emotionally up and down: high highs, angry lows.' The causes of this stress included 'failed music deals', Sevrin thinks. And, for all the charm and warmth we see in Steve today, even he admits he has a temper. In December 2008, *The Guardian* asked him in a Q&A, 'What is the trait you most deplore in yourself?' and he confessed, 'I'm not the nicest fella if I get angry.'

As for Sevrin's recollection of Steve's range of jobs, he said, 'A lot, yeah, I know he had done some carpentry when he was younger, but I never saw him doing anything but music-related things until I was in high school.' Now, we must bear in mind that Sevrin was only a toddler in the seventies, but did live with Steve again between the ages of thirteen and eighteen, so he was well placed not only to observe over many years, but to listen to family conversation about what else Steve had done. What Steve has said most recently about his working life has exaggerated the blue-collar jobs, and talked down everything else, and that includes both the music he seems to have been doing for most of the seventies and (to a lesser extent) eighties, and the one professional job that he certainly had for a couple of years while Sevrin was in high school.

Also, the degree of poverty that causes marriages to fracture and implode is only really explicable if Steve was travelling a lot, trying for musical work. As we can see from his work on vintage cars, motorbikes and tractors, or the fact that he was able to pick up carpentry work when he needed it, he was clearly a capable guy who could have found permanent work in one of those fields had he wanted to. It must have been the need to travel with touring bands – and be available for session work as guitarist and engineer – that meant he couldn't do these jobs full-time. A full-time mechanic or framer is nobody's idea of a rich man, but he earned enough in the seventies to look after a young family in modest comfort.

It's a baffling approach for Steve to take, talking down his musical career as he has done. For one thing, it doesn't seem plausible that a musician as accomplished as Steve could have sat on his hands for twenty-five years. He wouldn't have been as good as he was, when he broke through, if he hadn't been playing regularly in the meantime. As with his age, there is evidence directly attributable to Steve himself, lying around the Internet, in the public domain, that contradicts what he says. Is it some kind of bizarre marketing strategy, to make him appeal to a kind of *Top*

Gear audience, middle-aged, culturally and politically conservative, who wouldn't approve of a hippie musician leaving his kids and gigging? Why else would he say these things? It's not, as they say, very rock'n'roll.

In the end, the strain was too much for the marriage, and Steve left some time in 1980, hitting the road back to Europe. At that time Ivan was three and Sevrin five, and their relationship doesn't seem to have recovered, completely, especially for Ivan, who was younger, and spent even less time with his dad. 'Ivan has bad feelings for Dad because of how he left too many times. My brother stopped talking to my dad over me pretty much. I know he felt abandoned and replaced. We both did,' Sevrin reveals.

Sevrin and Steve remained close enough that Sevrin went back to live with Steve, Elisabeth (his second wife) and stepbrothers for some years in his teens, so he witnessed Steve as a dad to two sets of sons. It must have been a bittersweet experience, seeing Steve as an affectionate, hands-on dad the second time round. Sevrin spent quality time with Steve in his teens, helping to set up and run Moon Music in Olympia, which was first a guitar shop, then a guitar shop with a studio out the back and in due course a fully equipped studio that recorded Modest Mouse. He also attributes his love of music to Steve, even though Steve wasn't around enough to teach him much. 'I do credit him with the inspiration to be a musician, and he gave me both my first acoustic and my first electric guitar. Vocally encouraged – but only really taught me a couple riffs, I'm mostly self-taught. My mother and stepfather also both encouraged music and singing.'

Intriguingly, at the end of the SRF 3 Swiss TV interview with Steve in 2014, he describes his ambition for retirement as travelling the world visiting his grandchildren. That may of course be genuine – and there's no doubt from what Sevrin has said, as anyone would expect from his performances, that when things are going well Steve is a very warm and loving parent. One of Sevrin's more sour anecdotes, however, concerns the last time he saw Steve, sometime in late 2004, when Steve came to Washington State from Norway to visit Sevrin's daughter – Steve's granddaughter – on her fourth birthday. It wasn't so very long after Steve's heart attack, but all the same it hardly shows Steve in the light of a dedicated grandparent.

> I haven't seen him in twelve years or so and yeah we fought, kinda. He had just had his little heart attack and said that if I was so willing to get him worked up and angry then I must not care about him and stormed out of my house, on the first night he ever met my daughter, when she was four. I still chased him down and tried to apologise and gave him a ride to a hotel, but I never heard or saw him again. Again, I wasn't always easy to deal with, either, though.

When I asked whether Sevrin thought he would ever be back in touch with Steve, he replied, 'I really don't know, I tried a bunch to contact him but the old love turned cold . . . You can only hurt over someone so long. Him getting famous just made it harder to let go of him is all. But who knows, he might grow up some day? I know I haven't yet!'

SEASICK STEVE

It seems clear that, despite recent denials about the extent of his involvement with music in this period, it was Steve's dedication to his career that stretched the marriage to breaking point. The relationship with Victoria was now over for good; with Sevrin and Ivan, especially Sevrin, there were fun times to come, but also wounds that would heal only temporarily. Steve, meanwhile, did what he'd been doing most of his life: he picked up his guitar and hit the road.

CHAPTER 6

From Skelmerdale
to Nashville

The 1980s are another poorly documented period in Steve's life – but, such as it is, it makes for surprising reading. This period also contains one of the biggest mysteries of Steve's life, which leads onto a fascinating – and I believe, persuasive – conjecture. The events can only sketchily be established after Steve left Victoria, Sevrin and Ivan in 1980, went travelling with his guitar, and got to know Elisabeth Wold at a blues bar in the Norwegian capital, Oslo. Steve and Elisabeth got married in 1982, and at this point, Steve Leach became Steve Wold, although he carried on using the name 'Leach' for some professional purposes.

Who is Elisabeth? The short answer is: a very well-kept secret. I have not been able to find any photographs of her, either in print media or online. She is roughly the same age as Steve, but aside from that all we can say with certainty is that theirs shows every sign of being a very successful, close and balanced relationship. While she has been supportive of his musical career, to the point of chivvying him to record *Dog House Music* while he was recuperating from his heart attack, she also appears to have had more influence over Steve's career than Victoria. At the same time, it seems (we can't be certain) as though Steve sometimes attributes decisions to her when they were actually his.

One of the key problems with Steve's marriage to Victoria was the chronic lack of income, caused by his determined pursuit of musical work. Elisabeth seems to have taken a firmer line in this respect. Therefore, after a bit more travelling in the UK, the new couple returned to the USA. And there – although he doesn't like people knowing it – Steve became a respectable, educated, suburban, middle-class professional.

There's no record of Elisabeth's educational background. As far as we know, she has always done blue-collar jobs, but she obviously has a keen and well-informed interest in music and other arts, and possibly politics, of a hippie-ish hue similar to Steve's. This anecdote, which Steve told to *The Arts Desk* in June 2011, gives us some insight into both Elisabeth's line of work, and the very touching (for a twenty-five-year-old marriage) mutual care and concern between the two of them:

> I was with Warner-Atlantic for three years, something like that, but I only went with them for a certain reason . . . At the same time my wife was working at an old people's home. She was killing

herself and she didn't believe I was doing good so she wouldn't quit her job. It was actually hurting her. The only way she was going to quit this job was if I gave her a chunk of money so I sent out the idea that I may be available but I had no idea all these people wanted to sign me – but they did.

So I got this chunk of money and she still wouldn't quit her job. I signed to Warners and kind of lied to her a little bit. I got Andy [Zammit of Bronzerat Records] to call his friend, that guy from The Darkness, Dan [Hawkins], who had a little studio in Norfolk. I told my wife the record company was making me go to a studio, that I'd have to stay there for a few weeks and that I wouldn't do it unless she came along. They weren't making me do nothing really but she took two weeks' absence from work.

Now I could have made that record in two weeks but I said, 'Everything's going wrong, I need to take another two weeks,' so she took another two weeks absence. I stayed there a couple of months and spent a shit-load of money but she lost her job in the end. Once she'd been away from it five or six weeks she began to see how the job had been really killing her. I got myself into a bad deal but it was a good deal because she quit. For the most part she's come with me ever since.

Elisabeth seems to have had a decisive say in where the family lived throughout the marriage. Her desire to move to somewhere similar to Norway was apparently one of the factors in their move from Tennessee to Olympia, in the northwest. According to another fascinating report in local newspaper *Telen*, Elisabeth also had a role in choosing their home town in Norway, too, and for rather unexpected reasons. On 26 March 2001, *Telen* reported,

> The musician and studio owner from Seattle fell completely for the blues city in Telemark [Notodden]. During a road trip in Norway with his Norwegian wife Elisabeth in May last year Notodden was chosen. The reason why they settled on the city was not the blues festival, as one might think. Oh no. Steve's wife Elisabeth had read Dag Solstad's book *T. Singer* and wanted to swing by the city said Singer visited in the book. The result was love at first sight. In the summer Wold will move his family to Notodden. The bandwagon follows Steve's unique sound studio, which he now believes he has found a perfect location for.

As we saw in Chapter 2, Notodden's history as a blues city seemed, on the face of it, to be a decisive factor in the choice of location, and there is something a little tongue-in-cheek about this. It's too far-fetched a story to make up entirely, however, so there is likely to have been some truth in it. And Elisabeth's choice of reading matter gives an precious (if inconclusive) insight into an otherwise mysterious character.

Dag Solstad is widely regarded as one of Norway's most distinguished writers, and has won numerous awards in his home country. He is also ardently left-wing, and was heavily involved in the AKP, or Workers' Communist Party, a Marxist-Leninist organisation that was, in the late sixties and early seventies, committed to overthrowing the Norwegian government. After that movement failed, much of his fiction has explored the society and opinions of various kinds of revolutionary movements, sometimes in a humorous or satirical way.

The novel, *T. Singer*, which inspired Elisabeth to move to Notodden, is a lyrical, meditative and darkly comic study of relationships and isolation that opens in the early 1980s covers the following fifteen years or so. The protagonist, T. Singer himself, a thirty-four-year-old, newly qualified librarian, leaves Oslo and travels to Notodden to start a new life that is more satisfying than his life in the city, but anonymous. He marries single mother and ceramicist Merete Sæthre, but their relationship begins to turn sour. Some years later, Sæthre is killed in a car crash and he returns to Oslo with his stepdaughter, but they go on to live separately. Singer tries to define his identity through isolation rather than community, and eventually reaches a kind of curious satisfaction in being semidetached from society. Solstad received the Norwegian Critics' Prize for the third time for this novel, which remains one of his best-loved, combining both humour and serious philosophical debate. He has always expressed a scepticism about the potential for smothering complacency in the safety and stability of Norwegian society – which was one of his reasons for believing in revolution, at one point – and that scepticism is also present in this novel.

It would, of course, be unfair to ascribe Solstad's political views to Elisabeth Wold on the basis of her admiration for one of his less obviously political novels. However, it would probably be difficult to enjoy Solstad's work without at least some sympathy for some of his views, broadly expressed. And that does tally, to some extent, with what we've heard from Steve, both before and, to a lesser extent, after the 'Seasick Steve' era, that suggests he has a worldview much more experimental, liberal and far-out than we'd expect from someone wearing dungarees and a John Deere cap, who chats about vintage Chevvies with Jeremy Clarkson.

There are a few puzzles to unpick regarding Steve and Elisabeth's life before they returned to the USA. You would expect the new couple to have some fun before settling down, and it seems they went travelling in Europe for a bit. Yet what we know of their destinations is utterly baffling. For example, in 2006, Steve told bluesinlondon.com, 'And then in the eighties I lived in England for a little bit – I liked all them modern bands they were having back then. I lived near Kew Gardens for a little bit, then we went to live up Skelmersdale [Lancashire] for a while.'

Let's examine this reference to Kew first, while we scratch our heads about what the hell a couple looking for the musical highlights of Europe might want with Skelmersdale, one of the dullest of England's new towns. Steve's stay in Kew could easily have been musical work. That part of London has a rich musical heritage. Olympic Sound Studios – alongside Abbey Road one of London's most prestigious recording studios – was based in nearby Barnes from the late sixties until 2009, and was used by bands including the Rolling Stones, the Beatles, Jimi

Hendrix and Led Zeppelin. In 1981, Pete Townshend opened Eel Pie Studios in a converted boathouse on the Thames near Richmond, only a few miles from Kew. That studio would also have needed skilled engineers.

We've seen that Steve first met Led Zeppelin on his pizza-parlour tour with Lightnin' Hopkins in 1969, and he seems to have stayed in touch with Robert Plant. He told *The Arts Desk* in the same interview, 'I'll never forget that show. I went backstage and saw that Robert Plant was smoking English cigarettes. I'd never seen an English cigarette before in my life so I bummed one off him. That was my big claim. I now know Robert Plant quite well and I told him but he don't remember. It tasted like shit.' So it's possible that Steve picked up some studio or backing work through Plant – and, even if it wasn't directly his doing, by 1980 Steve was a much more experienced musician than he had been in 1969, with, it seems, much more experience with big bands in the late seventies than he lets on. And with the recording industry in sound financial health in the 1980s, it would have been quite easy for someone of his ability to pick up work in Kew (if not in Skelmersdale).

There's one more point of interest in Steve's statements. We've seen that he has completely airbrushed his first wife, Victoria, from his accounts of what he did in the seventies. But he tends to talk more openly about Elisabeth, and usually says so publicly if she was involved in some event. So does the statement 'I lived near Kew Gardens for a little bit, then we went to live up Skelmersdale' tell us something significant? If Kew was work, Steve may have lived in Kew alone, while Elisabeth continued working in

Norway for a few months, before they both went together to Skelmersdale.

So why Skelmersdale? Thankfully, the bluesinlondon. com interview was conducted before Steve's breakthrough, and he was more open with these details than he might be today. As he's concentrated more and more, post-*Hootenanny*, on the story of his hard-working life, the facts about his time in Skelmersdale – which if the (admittedly circumstantial) evidence is correct, represented a completely different kind of experience for him – have tended to disappear from his official biography. The strangest thing about Steve's comment is not that he should be in the UK to see modern bands – that's what he's been interested in his whole life – but the idea that anyone, at all, ever, would go to Skelmersdale for the music scene.

Had Steve decided to go to Manchester, and spent the eighties following the Smiths, New Order and Joy Division, we would immediately understand his remarks, and we'd hope that tapes still existed of Steve's duet with Morrissey. But Skelmersdale? Located roughly between Liverpool and Wigan in west Lancashire, it was originally one of Lancashire's long-disappeared mining towns. In 1961 it was designated a new town, intended for overspill population from a then crowded Liverpool. As industry in the area declined substantially during the 1970s, it became extremely run down, its only distinguishing feature a lot of roundabouts, like other new towns such as Milton Keynes. Perhaps, for an American (where they have only traffic lights), this was a draw?

Liverpudlians abbreviate the town's name to 'Skem',

pronounced to rhyme with 'phlegm', and rolled around the throat in much the same way. It would certainly have been a cheap place to live, but, as far as live culture was concerned, it would have been an absolute nonstarter. Nor is it a question of having to live somewhere cheap and commuting into a city. In 1980, there was no shortage of affordable accommodation in either Liverpool or Manchester.

Given that Steve had previously been spoiled by the cosmopolitan atmospheres of San Francisco and Paris, and the exotic vibe of Hawaii, there would have to be a very special reason why he would go somewhere that is such an embodiment of suburban drabness. And, if the 'we' in Steve's quotation does indeed imply he was with Elisabeth in Skelmersdale, there would have to be an even more special reason why he'd take his new partner there. Steve was thirty in 1981, of course, with no qualifications and an employment record best described as patchy. By the mid-1980s, at the latest, the couple were both established in the USA, and Steve had settled down – probably with some encouragement from Elisabeth, since he had been disinclined to take on a suburban career while he had been married to Victoria.

When I first began researching Steve's connection with Skelmersdale, it struck me as both bizarre and baffling. His trip to Hawaii could just have been a holiday, but this dismal, wet, music-free place? Of course, once Steve's connection with Shanti is established, the answer that suggested itself (although it's, admittedly, still circumstantial) becomes obvious. Given the date of Steve and Elisabeth's visit to Skelmersdale (some time in 1980–2), this is why I suggest they went there. This is how the institution is described on its own website:

> Maharishi European Sidhaland was established in Skelmersdale, Lancashire, in 1980, as a place for those interested in the practice of Transcendental Meditation and living an ideal, healthy quality of life. It was created through the inspiration of Maharishi Mahesh Yogi, founder of Transcendental Meditation (TM), and is dedicated to individual enlightenment for its members and creating world peace through the positive influence of collective practice of these programmes.
>
> At the heart of this community is the Golden Dome, the purpose-built facility for this group practice of Transcendental Meditation, the TM-Sidhi programme and Yogic Flying. In the 35 years that the Maharishi European Sidhaland has been in existence, approximately 1,610,035 meditations have taken place either in the Dome or in facilities used before the Dome was built, an average of 46,001 per year!

I have managed to track down one couple who were active in the Transcendental Meditation community in Skelmersdale in the early 1980s. They don't recall Steve and Elisabeth, but, then again, they were there thirty-five years ago, and there are 46,000 meditations a year, so tracing one couple is a needle-and-haystack business.

It's intriguing that Steve should wish to introduce

Elisabeth to Transcendental Meditation – assuming that this is why they were in Skelmersdale – so soon after their initial meeting. It may imply that Elisabeth, having missed out on Steve's experiences in San Francisco (Oslo was cosmopolitan by Norwegian standards, but no San Francisco), was keen to catch up and experience the same things that he had. It probably also tells us that enthusiasm for TM was an important feature of one of Steve's partners. Since Elisabeth, like Victoria, travelled to Hawaii to give birth, presumably at a TM centre, much later, in 1988, the habit must have stuck. We will probably never know whether Elisabeth knew Victoria had also been to Hawaii with Steve to give birth. It's a pattern not all wives would be happy to continue – most mothers-to-be would surely prefer to make their own arrangements about something as personal as childbirth. Even in 1988, then, the balance of probability is that TM was still an important part of both Steve's and Elisabeth's life.

Returning to the USA probably in 1982, the couple were married. It was probably necessary for them to be married to enable Elisabeth to live in the United States (which helps us to date their return), though there's no doubt it was primarily a love match. From this point on, Steve began – selectively – to use Elisabeth's surname, Wold. The name seems to have been confined to his musical identity, for he continued to be known as Leach in his non-musical life for another twenty years. For example, there was a mention of Steve in an article published in the Norwegian national newspaper *Dagbladet* on 23 September 2002. It concerned the debut album from the then twenty-five-year-old Vidar

Vang. Entitled *Rodeo*, the LP was recorded at Steve's studio, Juke Joint. The piece states,

> Steve Wold (51) is a cunning American who has played with Joni Mitchell, the Beach Boys and the Grateful Dead. Actually his name was Leach, but he married a Norwegian woman twenty years ago and took her name. Last year the family moved from the US to Notodden. Wold is passionate about analogue and there is hardly a digital device in the studio. On the old Stax equipment he has captured the unkempt nerve in Vang's music.

The attitude of awe and respect shown to Steve at this point by the Norwegian music community is intriguing. The Norwegian word for 'cunning' is *'ringrev'*, which is most literally translated as 'fox', or even 'salty dog'!

What happened next definitely happened – but it's been frustratingly hard to prove exactly when and where it actually took place. It's extraordinary this story has been unreported, even though it's still publicly available on a well-known website. Perhaps Steve has been in touch with the author of the post (whom he seems to have known well at some point) and explained that his contributions to public debate are not welcome. Reading the following on Yahoo! Answers – which was still published at the time of writing – provided one of many eureka moments in my research. It's one of many substantial dents in Steve's version of his career. The writer – Joe, from Tennessee – states,

> I knew Steven Leach in the 90's and he was married

The now classic 'Seasick Steve' pose: head thrown back and howling his blues to the sky.

Above left: Seasick Steve at the 2007 Mojo Awards, where he won the Best Breakthrough Act award following his appearance on Jools Holland's 2006 *Hootenanny*.

Above right: Steve on stage at Glastonbury 2007. He played at more UK festivals in this year than any other artist.

Below: Steve also keeps up a ferocious work ethic when touring the continent. Pictured here signing a fan's shoe at the Crossing Borders Festival in the Netherlands, in 2008.

Above: Steve returns to his roots in 2008, busking in the Paris Métro.

Below: …but draws a much larger crowd in 2009 at London's Earls Court tube station a year later, after being nominated for Best International Male Solo Artist at the Brit Awards.

Above: Steve hosting the 2009 'Hollerers, Stompers & Old-Time Ramblers' session of the London Barbican's Folk America event. Note his own clothes on the washing line behind him – a theme he repeated on his very first full-length gig, in a music bar in Norway in 2003.

Below left: In 2011, Steve played the iconic main stage at Reading Festival, touting perhaps the most unusual guitar that hallowed arena has ever seen.

Below right: A rare shot of Steve with his wife Elisabeth, in London.

Since his breakout, Steve's rootsy style and renegade image have attracted collaborations with some of the biggest names in music. Pictured here playing with similarly offbeat blues-rock superstar Jack White and Alison Mosshart of The Dead Weather (above), as well as singer Paloma Faith and John Paul Jones of Led Zeppelin fame (below). Steve and Jones are regular collaborators.

Above: Above: Steve playing The Three-String Trance Wonder (or, 'The Biggest Piece of Shit in the World' as it is affectionately known…).

Below: To add to the roster of what must be one of the oddest guitar collections in the world, Steve sports his hubcap guitar complete with broomstick neck at V Festival in 2013. He cheerfully describes it as 'like playing with a piece of dynamite', owing to its proclivity to break in the middle of a performance.

Above: Playing with his son Paul in London. Paul has joined Steve on stage many times and also does guitar tech work for him.

Below: Prominently displaying the Mississippi license plate underneath a one-string cigar box guitar in Belfort, France.

to Elisebeth [*sic*] (from Norway) and had children. He lived in Franklin Tennessee just outside of Nashville. He worked as a Paramedic. I worked with him for several years. He moved to Seattle to be a Paramedic, which was the last we had seen of him. If you do a license search in Seattle you will not find a Paramedic with the name Steven Leach, but interestingly enough you will find a Steven G. Wold that was in Seattle just when Steve Leach left Tennessee.

Steve was a very talented musician and one day one of the guys at work stumbled onto seasick [*sic*] Steve on the internet and recognized him as Steven Leach even after the fact that it had been over 20 years since we had seen him. His name change was new to us as well as his biography posted on the internet. He was a good paramedic and had no tales of traveling around homeless. I believe in his talent as I witnessed it and love him for that. I was not aware that he needed to change his name as his life was very normal from what we saw of him. This has been a mystery to us.

This was actually posted as an answer, apparently only two years ago, to the question 'Why did "Seasick Steve" take his wife's name when he married her in 1982?' Underneath is the note, 'It's unusual for a man to take his wifes [*sic*] name upon marriage, I wonder what the motivation [was] for Steven Gene Leach to change his name to Steven Gene Wold upon marrying his current wife in 1982?' This seems more pointed a question than Joe's answer, listing Steve's full name and being phrased in a somewhat exaggeratedly innocent manner. Joe's answers sounds slightly baffled and hurt at the apparent deception of a one-time friend, but written purely in a spirit of discovering the truth, even though, almost certainly without meaning to, it drives a coach and horses through the key tenets of the accepted biography of 'Seasick Steve'.

The first thing to note is that Steve is indeed a trained paramedic, and what Joe says about the records in Seattle is true. Unfortunately, the relevant records for Tennessee, which Steve and his family left in 1991 (probably), are no longer available in public – at least online. But search the Washington State database for a paramedic called Steven Gene Wold, born 1951, and you will find a Paramedic Certification listing, with a licence number ES 00129966, which was issued on 31 December 1995, and expired on 30 April 1996. This is an official US state record, and unless there is another paramedic with exactly the same name and birthday, and everything Joe says is a malicious prank, there is no doubt, even on this evidence, that Steve was a certified paramedic.

It was also confirmed by Sevrin Johnson, Steve's son, independently. In order not to ask a leading question, I phrased my enquiry as openly as possible: 'What sort of work was he doing when you were young? Was it all studio work?' Sevrin replied, 'A lot, yeah, I know he had done some carpentry when he was younger but I never saw him doing anything but music-related things until I was in high school, and then for a brief time he was a paramedic until he hurt his back on the job. I think he only did that for a few years.' Sevrin would have been a high-school freshman in 1988, which would give the years 1988–91 as the term of Steve's Tennessee paramedic career.

This just about fits in with the timing Joe gives in his post: if Joe last saw Steve in 1991, and the post was written in 2013, that explains the reference to 'over 20 years' ago. If Steve suffered a back injury from the heavy lifting involved in emergency medical work – in, say, 1991 – he still maintained his qualification, just in case, for another five years until it expired in 1996. A very prudent approach to his professional career.

To train to be a paramedic in the USA takes between one and two years, though Steve would also have had to obtain some kind of GED (General Educational Development) qualification, because he had not originally graduated from high school. Not only that: he had probably completed only about a year of high school, so he had a lot of catching up to do. Sevrin reckons Steve 'did just over two years in Tennessee for paramedic school', which means he must have started studying sometime in 1985. The fact that he was able to do this, and then go on to qualify in a highly technical, responsible and moderately scientific profession, suggests a capacity for formal learning far beyond anything he's admitted to in public. Steve's college degree would be public information, and I have made enquiries about it with a number of colleges near Nashville – so far without success. I suspect Steve studied at Columbia State College, southwest of Nashville, which has proved particularly difficult to contact. It would have been helpful to know the exact dates of Steve's qualification. However, given the Washington State record, which is public and official, he must have completed a college qualification.

His ability is, of course, entirely unsurprising. With no formal training and only intermittent, on-the-job teaching, he has taught himself both guitar and sound engineering (which requires a similar balance of technical competence and people skills) to a highly professional standard. There is also evidence he had his first professional studio in Tennessee before he set up Moon Studios in Olympia. He may even have started before he went to college, deciding to train to be a paramedic because the Tennessee studio didn't work out for him. So, on and off, he ran a professional recording studio for twenty years, between Tennessee and Notodden, and, although only the Olympia studio can be considered an out-and-out success, no one has ever suggested the others failed because he wasn't a good engineer. Those studios were simply in the wrong place at the wrong time, and Steve didn't have the contacts necessary to build up business. In short, this is not the background of an uneducated drifter.

Steve would probably say that he didn't work as a paramedic for all that long. Perhaps he did it to help raise money for studio equipment, or for the family to move to Olympia once Tennessee no longer became viable as a studio destination. All the same, it does radically change the standard impression of his life as 'Seasick Steve', and show that this is another area of his biography in which he has been more than a little misleading – witness Steve's remark, to *The Arts Desk*, in response to a question about his oldest son:

> He's a physicist. His name's Henry. He has a band. Last year he came out on the road with us taking care of the drums but now he's just done his Masters in physics. I think he's going to do a doctorate now. He's real smart. If he didn't look so much like me I'd want to do a DNA test and make sure we was related.

Steve the paramedic, with his college qualification, is too self-effacing with such a comment. Likewise, the lyric 'I didn't have me no real school education, so what in the hell what I was gonna be able to do?', from 'Dog House Boogie', simply can't be true – and the answer to what he 'was gonna be able to do', is actually quite a lot. He is not directly responsible for some of the wilder interpretations of his image – witness the following profile on website thecountryblues.com – but he has allowed a misleading picture of his past to build up, and such over-the-top passages are the consequence:

> Seasick isn't dressing up for an act. He is the real deal. He isn't an impostor who learned the blues from records. He was a throw-away teenager, who lived in the mean streets and survived the hard way, best described in his song 'I was born with nothing and still have most of it left' [*sic*]. Much can be and much has been said about his hobo-cruising,

train-hopping, fruit picking, hard intoxicating, jail-
bird, song-and-dance man existence . . . Naturally,
all that makes good fodder for the blues, even for
a white boy. Indeed, that sad life gave Seasick a
lifetime of song material and a dysfunctional life.
No education, no stability, no security, no 9 to 5,
none of the problems of middle-class suburbia.
Instead, he made it on the tough streets on the edge
of mainstream in the counterculture.

The last two sentences in this passage are – in light of what
we've learned – ridiculous. What Steve has done is what
many musicians have to do: work hard over a long period
of time to gain recognition. He had to work for longer
than most, but then the recognition, when it came, arrived
in a spectacular avalanche. He has shown an amazingly
imaginative insight into a kind of reimagined roots music
that is raw and new, and still a bit rough round the edges,
with tales that can move anyone. That doesn't make the
tales true, though.

On that subject, Joe's comment on Yahoo! Answers that
Steve 'had no tales of traveling around homeless' ties in
with Sevrin's description of the hobo stories as a 'gimmick',
and what we have already seen about the biographical
impossibility of 'eleven years of bumblin' around and livin'
kinda hand-in-mouth'. It's more shocking to hear that Steve
had exactly the kind of mundane, suburban, middle-class
existence of which his career seems the antithesis. In some
ways, this line is the most shocking – from one middle-class
professional to another: 'I was not aware that he needed

to change his name as his life was very normal from what
we saw of him.' Knowledge of Steve's professional career
changes how we may regard other important episodes,
too. For example, he often praises his wife's response to his
heart attack, suggesting that Elisabeth saved his life because
she was the one who identified the symptoms. Of course,
having a loved one present in such circumstances is a huge
comfort, and her role was obviously very important both
practically and emotionally. Yet spotting and treating heart
attacks is in many ways a paramedic's most important job.
It seems surprising that he knew as little about what was
happening as he lets on in this account given to *The Daily
Mail* in January 2009:

> It was there that Steve suffered his heart attack.
> Were it not for Elizabeth's [*sic*] quick thinking, he
> says, he wouldn't be here now.
>
> 'I was in serious shape,' he shudders. 'It all
> happened in the middle of the night. I felt as if
> someone had suddenly thrust a spear into my
> chest. Luckily, we were only ten minutes from the
> hospital. If we'd been another 15 minutes away, I
> don't think I'd have pulled through. 'Elizabeth [*sic*]
> was in bed with me and she knew straight away
> what was going on. She called the ambulance and
> they fixed me up. It was all pretty horrible.'

Based on the reports from Steve's son Sevrin and Joe of
Yahoo! Answers, the family were living at this time just
outside the city of Franklin, about ten miles southwest of

Nashville. We hardly need ask what brought Steve to the place widely known as 'Music City'. But the local scene is not especially one associated with Steve: Nashville is famous as the centre of the country, bluegrass and hillbilly music scene, popularised by the long-running *Grand Ole Opry* radio show. Although Steve has recorded a country song - 'Purple Shadows', on *Hubcap Music* - and has sometimes acknowledged a debt to country music (witness his comment to *The Arts Desk* in 2011: 'I always thought I played hillbilly music'), his own music is indebted to the blues above all else. In particular, the glossy, processed sound that characterises much contemporary country music is the opposite end of the spectrum from Steve's gruff, DIY aesthetic.

It's always difficult to draw generic distinctions that are both broad and meaningful, but there are clear differences between the blues - descended from an African slave heritage and brought into Memphis from the South - and country music, largely derived from European folk traditions and brought to Nashville from the North and East. One of the features that give Tennessee, in particular, such a rich musical heritage is its position on the dividing line where these traditions meet. It's appropriate, then, that Steve - born a middle-class white boy, but with a black musical upbringing - should have lived there for nearly a decade.

However, there are probably other developments that brought Steve to Nashville, and made Music City, for a while, the perfect spot for one of his studios. We'll see in the next chapter how dedicated Steve was in his pre-fame years to the idea of an independent music scene, in which the control of major labels was very limited, and within which small bands could forge their own way by playing in independent venues. Independent recording studios are also an essential part of that kind of scene, as Steve was later to demonstrate with Moon Studios in Olympia. And, though he eventually did succumb to the temptation of a relatively secure middle-class career, it probably wasn't until he'd attempted a musical career first.

There are a couple of hints on record that Steve's first studio may have been in Tennessee, and not Olympia. He has kept quiet about this, usually stating that he began producing and recording professionally only after the family had moved to Washington State in 1990s. In 2006, he told bluesinlondon.com, 'I'd learnt how to do music engineering in the late sixties, being a technician or coffee maker or whatever in a studio, so could fall back on that kind of a job. I started buying pieces of equipment so I could build my own studio some day. Then we moved to Tennessee again, making some recordings there, but I got sick of being there . . .'

There's a little more detail about this Tennessee studio in the press release published by Neuland Concerts to promote *Man From Another Time* in 2009: 'Moving to rural Tennessee he built a small recording studio, but when that didn't work out "because there was this whole country and western, Christian bullshit thing goin' on down there," the Wolds eventually had to pack up and leave again. This time, on account of the fact that Mrs Wold was pining for the fjords – "she just wanted to live someplace that looked like Norway" – they chose to head north to Washington State, on the North Western seaboard.'

Intriguingly, the only other mention of Steve being involved with a studio before Moon Studios in Olympia occurs in an interview he gave to Seattle magazine *The Stranger* in December 2000, just before he left for Norway, in which he gives what we can only assume to be a deliberately misleading account of his Tennessee studio experience:

> Wold began recording local bands shortly after he and his family moved from Europe – where he'd been running a studio – to Olympia in 1991. Whatever Wold's immediate plans had been at the time of relocation, they didn't include opening up another studio, at least not professionally. 'I got sick of recording,' he says. 'It had been a few years, because I had sold my studio in Europe and I wasn't going to do it again.'

For one thing, the family didn't move from Europe in 1991: they moved from Tennessee. And there's no evidence he'd ever owned a studio in Europe: he'd never had the money, or stayed in one place long enough, apart from Paris (and he definitely didn't have a studio there). For another thing, according to Sevrin (as we shall see next chapter), Steve began collecting the lo-fi studio gear that eventually fitted out Moon Studios pretty much straightaway after they'd moved to Olympia, so he can't have been that fed up with recording.

In fact, engineering work is something he has turned to,

again and again, from his teens until he sold Juke Joint in Notodden in 2005. And, even then, he saved a tape recorder, and produced *Dog House Music* for himself. Recording is obviously in his blood. Otherwise, on the face of it, it's a baffling statement. Perhaps Steve didn't want to be rude about the Christian movement he felt had impeded his Tennessee studio. Yet he was about to leave the country, and never wanted the Christian musicians' patronage anyway, so it's difficult to imagine he'd have been bothered about ruffling some pious feathers.

Why Tennessee, though? For a start, it has a thriving blues scene, and Steve has been associated with one of Tennessee's most distinguished bluesmen – indeed, one of the greatest guitarists of all time. In an interview with the webzine earpollution.com given shortly after Steve left Olympia for Norway (there's no published date, but late 2001 seems most likely), Steve's friends the Tremens allude to the range of acts Steve had known or worked with, mentioning that he had played with guitarist Albert King. Steve, of course, won't say anything about such an occasion. It must have taken place while Steve was living near Nashville. Albert King died in 1992, and was ill for some time beforehand, so it can't have been after Steve left in 1991. King lived a few hours away in Memphis, and is known to have performed in Nashville, so this seems to be the obvious occasion. The following report, from the cleveland.com website, dates from April 2013. It relates to King's induction in the Cleveland-based Rock and Roll Hall of Fame that year and gives us a sense of King's presence and priorities as a musician. Cincinnati blues guitarist Kelly

SEASICK STEVE

Richey (dubbed the 'female Stevie Ray Vaughan') played with Albert King at the Cuckoo Club in Nashville in 1988:

'The word attitude doesn't really serve a great enough purpose. Albert King embodied the blues,' Richey said. 'Every note he played sang. He was one with his guitar and his vocal instrument. As a guitarist and vocalist, he was in command.'

In fact, such was King's command that he got Vaughan to sing, she said.

'Albert made Stevie Ray get in front of a mike,' Richey said. 'Without him, that might not have happened.'

King pushed her and others to focus on the vocals, not just being a hotshot guitarist, she said.

'Stevie Ray and Jimi, you never would have known them if they'd just been singers. But you wouldn't know them as well if they'd just been guitarists, either.'

Richey said King didn't see it as a choice.

'To him, it's just what you're supposed to do. Guitar's part of the equation. But singing is, too. You have to learn to sing to make your guitar sing as well. And oh, good Lord, could he sing. He could sing with mouth open or fingers flying.'

King had immense stage charisma. His musical style was different from Steve's, with a powerful, thrusting kind of playing that in some ways is the opposite of Steve's generally more reflective and wistful manner. King's choice of guitar, the Flying V, is so heavy you have to stand to manage the weight, whereas Steve's often makeshift instruments are built to be caressed in his lap. Yet, as an example of how to unite form and content, style and performance, and play with total conviction, King must have been an inspiration:

> While the runs, fills and chording may be difficult to replicate, Richey sees King's legacy, passing from generation to generation of blues guitarists, as something less tangible, but far more important, than any technical aspect will ever be.
>
> 'Every note Stevie Ray played, he poured everything into it. That came from Albert. And that's the kind of player I am.
>
> 'The blues may not be complicated, but it isn't easy. Lifting boulders isn't complicated, it's hard work. The blues is the same way.'
>
> Perhaps it's with a respect for that work in mind that King warned Richey not to trifle with the blues.
>
> 'Albert said to me, "If you pick up a guitar, it's a like a pistol," Richey remembered. 'You best mean to use it.'

Since Steve was in Tennessee for nearly a decade, they may well have met many more times than once. We can't say exactly how much of Steve's experience with King rubbed off in any meaningful way, but there are significant points of comparison between the two, and Steve, in his thirties throughout the 1980s, was young enough to learn new tricks. It's also possible that Steve at least heard, if not played with – he'd probably have been too young – Albert King in 1967 at the Fillmore in San Francisco. King's breakthrough album on Stax, *Born Under a Bad Sign* was released that year, and King sold out both the East and West Fillmore venues many times.

Overall, Albert King sounds like a more conventional blues-rocker than Steve does, albeit an incredibly skilful and sonorous one. However, there are many features of his playing that may have been cultivated or influenced by playing time with Albert King. Firstly, virtuosity: watching inspirational people perform at an astonishing level is always an effective motivator, and Steve's guitar-playing clearly came on since noodling rather ponderously on bass in the Shanti performance of 1971 referred to earlier. By 2001, as the Tremens say in their interview in *Ear Pollution*, Steve's 'a fucking awesome guitar player'.

But Steve, like Albert King, is not all about guitar. The Tremens also say (referring, in fairness, to a different vocal project) that his 'voice sounds like Joe Cocker'. A Seasick Steve performance is an inseparable blend of voice and guitar, the grit and sweetness of his voice steadying the dizzying acrobatics on guitar. In terms of matching vocal and guitar-playing skill, then, Steve and King are together all the way, as they also are on the guitar-as-pistol approach. There are very few artists with the same punch Steve can give to performance when he puts his mind to it.

Like Albert King, Steve isn't bothered about genre boundaries. Rather, as the 'song-and-dance man' he likes to claim to be, he understands that entertainment comes first, and technical boundaries second. King was always rooted in the blues, but at various times incorporated both funk and soul into his act, according to the musical demands of the day.

Finally, there is some common ground in the musical priorities of both artists. King's most memorable performances, like Steve's, were songs that told a story, with realistic details about a hard life. He recorded several versions of Blind Lemon Jefferson's 'Matchbox Blues' – about a relationship breaking up, and the man packing his possessions into a matchbox before leaving – and each time makes a point of telling the story very clearly, alongside the guitar pyrotechnics. King's 1967 album *Born Under a Bad Sign*, meanwhile, is one of the landmark albums of modern blues, and was hugely influential on a generation of performers (especially Clapton and Hendrix) for the way it combined technical virtuosity with a fluid and energetic approach to the genre that breathe new life into a music that was beginning to be overshadowed by rock and roll. In that sense, Steve's punk-blues breakthrough forty years later, though the sound is different, could be said to have saved the music for another generation with a similar rejuvenation of traditional styles.

Unlike Steve, King was just about old enough to see the hardship of the Deep South, and began his life picking cotton in Arkansas, so (although he left the fields for professional music as a young man) he had a glimpse of what the hard physical labour of the original blues singers was like. Steve, we may say, escaped the physical hardship, but had to wait a lot longer than his talent deserved for a musical breakthrough.

Steve's use of customised guitars and unconventional instruments such as the diddley bow seems mainly to date from after the creation of his 'Seasick' alter ego in 2003 (and as such, I would argue, is open to a degree of sceptical speculation about its authenticity), so in that sense he took advantage of the technical opportunities of playing single-stringed instruments in the reverse way from Albert King, who started on them, but went on to play a Gibson Flying V for most of his career. However, he clearly knows how to make these instruments sing. And, according to a new article (January 2016) in *Guitar Player* magazine, King's unusual technique may have originated in the use of his home-made cigar-box guitar.

> Albert King induced Lucy, his Gibson Flying V, to moan and cry the blues. He played left-handed and upside down, and the massively bent notes arced from his strings as he yanked them down with his fingers. In an African-American tradition going back to the one-stringed diddley bows, King squeezed out fluid microtones as expressive as the melismatic singing found in field hollers.
>
> Born Albert Nelson on April 25 1923, in Indianola, Mississippi, King acquired the surname of his stepfather. Seeing the legendary Blind Lemon Jefferson perform in the late Thirties inspired him to make a cigar-box guitar.

On diddley bow, and even on a regular guitar, Steve's use of microtones and slide is exceptionally skilful. There is a great example of this in his song 'Levee Camp Blues', available as an extra on the special edition of *I Started Out With Nothin . . .* (or on YouTube, recorded at one of his Barbican shows). As he plays an old acoustic guitar, with a metal slide tube on his wedding ring finger, his voice (though very effective in the context) doesn't quite have the mystical, quavering quality of a Son House or Blind Lemon Jefferson, but the 'melismatic singing' of his slide playing, to borrow *Guitar Player*'s excellent phrase, is spine-shiveringly evocative, and the occasional buzz from his clapped-out instrument only adds to the mood.

Although the extent to which this was learned from Albert King is of course debatable, the two men clearly have the same kind of technical skill deriving directly from the earliest African-American music. And the fact that they played together, perhaps many times, and lived in the same state for ten years, fleshes out our picture of Steve's musical development in these otherwise rather mysterious years.

Steve's voice in 'Levee Camp Blues', though more accessible to a modern audience than the quintessential Jefferson whine, still brings an authentically desolate, yearning quality, entirely in keeping with the character of the piece. One of the most impressive features of Steve's playing is the way he is able to draw on techniques from blues history and, if they work, employ them in a context where they don't sound hidebound or archaic.

It wasn't just the promise of established blues stars that drew Steve to Tennessee, however. Starting in the early eighties, just before he and his family arrived, and lasting for six or seven years, Nashville had a vigorous and exciting independent music scene, driven in the first instance by punk fans, and in many ways very like that which Steve found in Olympia ten years later. YouTube channel nashville80srock has some entertaining footage of the time. It started, in 1980, with a country record employee called Rick Champion, who'd got into punk, and was frustrated that he couldn't get the LPs locally. Having a beer one night at the basement bar Phrank 'n' Steins (recalled by some as Phranks 'n' Steins), Campion was struck by the fact that the space would be perfect for rock gigs, so, in January 1980, he began programming the venue, and Nashville's first punk-rock club was born. The story was told to *Nashville Scene* magazine in 2006:

> The impact was immediate. Nashville's first punk band, Cloverbottom – named after the local mental hospital – formed shortly thereafter, led by Johnny Hollywood on bass and Rock Strata on guitar. Others, like the Electric Boys and Jap Sneakers, seemed to spring up as soon as they got wind of the club. Groups like the Ratz began playing regularly, stoking their sets with Ramones covers, while other punk acts such as USR had more political bite. There was now a place and a sound for this growing scene of kids hungry for anything with three wee chords and a whole lotta rage.
>
> 'Suddenly, these little punkoid high school kids started crawling out of the woodwork,' Champion says. The club pulled in people like Barry 'Cheetah' Feltz, self-styled leader of a rat pack in chains and

black leather who called themselves the 'Belleview Crew.' Dave Willie, singer for Committee for Public Safety and the dark late-'80s art-pop band Jet Black Factory, remembers sneaking into the club as a high school student.

"[It was a] small scene and everyone knew each other,' says Willie, who with CPS helped entice bands like Minor Threat and Black Flag to Nashville. 'I was thrilled to find it. It seemed like the perfect vehicle for confrontation and rebellion.'

And it wasn't just obscure young punk bands who started out at Phranks. REM made their Nashville debut there later in 1980 for a $100 guarantee and door money. Phranks itself didn't last that long. There were the usual problems that beset a new scene – expanding at a faster rate than it can easily manage, with underage drinking and drug use – and it was forced to close later that year. But the demand for an independent music venue in Nashville was still growing, and another club – Cantrell's (named after its owner Terry Cantrell) and more than twice the size of Phranks – opened as soon as the latter had shut down. Cantrell's gave independent bands a platform for five years until it, too, shut, after which the indie character of Nashville music stalled a little, for a variety of reasons. The stranglehold of country music was gone for good, however.

The first Nashville indie band to raise a flag for the local scene were the White Animals, a quartet recording exclusively on their own Dread Beat label. Although they never signed to a major label, their blend of psychedelia, dub and punk was popular with college radio. Their videos were early MTV hits. Bands such as Jason and the (Nashville) Scorchers, playing a blend of indie rock and country, emerged in 1981, and were so well reviewed that they were signed to EMI in 1983, on the condition they drop the 'Nashville' from their name. It was a lose–lose situation: local fans were offended, but the band still didn't really fit into either rock or country radio profiles, and struggled to gain the airtime they needed to build an audience. Eventually, they were dropped again by EMI in 1987. By 1985, the peak of Nashville's new independent music-making, record-label A&R people were regularly found checking out the talent.

A 1983 TV series entitled *Nashville New Wave* (available on YouTube) gives invaluable footage and some interviews with these bands. They weren't punk in a pure sense, but imported punk's attitude to a usually more acoustic, country music-based foundation. By the time Steve returned to the USA (probably) in 1982 to marry Elisabeth, there was enough independent music being made in Nashville to draw Steve to Music City to build a career – certainly for someone with as finely tuned an ear for an exciting new scene as Steve.

Why was Steve interested in a punk-influenced scene? We know from many remarks he has made that he felt the blues was dying. We know that he was attracted to the energy and anarchy of punk. He has described vividly his first experience of seeing a punk gig, almost by accident, in the seventies, in an interview with *The Independent* in September 2008: 'I just turned around and got in line. And it was an Iggy Pop show. That was the first punk I'd seen. I walked out a different person. That boy rearranged my brain cells.' Some of the bands he recorded in Olympia in the nineties (Kathleen Hanna and Kill Rock Stars, for example) were part of the broader punk heritage. There's a strand of punk in his own act: he's described as a 'punk blues' singer in his iTunes biography, and widely elsewhere. Given that Steve was keen to establish himself in a thriving music scene, the most likely explanation for the family's decision to live in Nashville is that Steve identified it as a growing independent music scene, and hoped it would be a good source of studio and engineering work.

A plausible timescale for this decade would be as follows. Given that while the paramedic qualification is definite, and the studio very likely, we don't know exactly when either happened. If we accept Sevrin's account that Steve was working full-time at music until about 1988, when he began working as a paramedic, it would suggest that the initial plan was for Steve to work full-time as an engineer and backing guitarist (as he did when recording Modest Mouse in 1990s) when the family moved to Tennessee. The Nashville indie scene declined with the closure of Cantrell's in 1986, and this is when Steve began paramedic training and started work in 1988. This would then fit with the timescales outlined by both Sevrin and Joe of Yahoo! Answers, while also matching both Steve's interests, and the rise and fall of indie music in Nashville. It would also allow for a gap of three years between Steve's Tennessee studio and the beginnings of Moon Music in Olympia, as he said he wanted in his interview with *The Stranger*.

SEASICK STEVE

As for the role of 'this whole country and western, Christian bullshit thing goin' on down there' in the failure of Steve's studio, to blame country music for the failure of a Nashville studio seems a bit bizarre – rather like setting up a studio in New Orleans and complaining about the jazz. The Christian element in the quote is more interesting, though. Today, there are dozens of radio stations in the area that describe themselves as 'Christian Contemporary', 'Southern Gospel' or something along similar lines. Exploring the history of these a little reveals that many were originally non-religious music stations that went bust, and were bought by a religious broadcasting company of some kind.

For example, WNQM, or Nashville Quality Ministries, now a Christian station owned by FW Robert Broadcasting, was originally founded by a Texas newspaper publisher in 1945 as a popular music station. It broadcast a mixture of rock, country and disco, until it closed in 1983, and reopened as a religious station in 1984. WVRY, another Tennessee station that originally broadcast a Top 40 show, has since begun broadcasting religious fare (although in this case not until after Steve left the state). Likewise, WENO, an AM broadcaster with a historically important role in country music broadcasting, went bust in the early 1980s and is now a gospel music station. Many Christian stations can draw on listeners' donations to assist their running costs in a way that secular music stations cannot, and they also have a middle-class, middle-aged listener demographic that is attractive to advertisers. Indie music fans, however discerning their taste, are often young, relatively less well off, and less suggestible to mainstream advertising for cat food, processed cheese and car insurance. Radio airtime would have been a crucial part of building an audience for a new release (these days, with social media, it's less crucial), and, if the stations Steve needed to support his record releases were being bought up by Christian broadcasters, he may have had a point about the 'Christian bullshit thing'.

Steve's family life at this time sounds pretty idyllic. His first two children with Elisabeth – Henry James Wold and Didrik – were born in Franklin, but their personal information is very closely protected, so their true birth dates are not known. They were probably born between 1982 and 1988. Henry, who has a co-producing credit for *You Can't Teach An Old Dog New Tricks*, and played drums on *Dog House Music*, is now the physics teacher in Norway whose DNA Steve has joked about testing. Didrik is a graphic designer and illustrator, who has created most of Steve's album artwork.

Youngest son Paul Martin Wold was born in Hawaii – like Steve's second son, Ivan – in 1988. Was the location linked to Steve's interest in Transcendental Meditation? We can't prove it, but it seems likely. BBC Radio Lancashire conducted an interview with him in January 2010 (still available online), tied to the launch of his debut album *A Waste of Time Well Spent*. He confirms the details of his birth, explaining that his family was in Hawaii for six months in total. The date fits in with the likely end of Steve's paramedic studies, so perhaps they all went there to celebrate. We know no more. Paul Martin is the most musical of the three:

he has his own career, as well as performing on stage with Steve, and sometimes works as his father's guitar tech.

Paul Martin has a rather different take on the experience of being Steve's son from that of Sevrin. In the BBC story accompanying the interview, he gives his views on Steve's parenting skills:

> What is it like being the son of the blues legend? 'Throughout my life he's always been the best father I could ever ask for, and I'm so happy for him now he's achieved success doing what he loves. It's what we all dream of really, and he finally got his break.

Sevrin, who lived with Steve and Elisabeth during high school (from 1988 to 1993), drew a distinction between his own experiences of Steve as a father and those of his youngest three brothers from Steve's second marriage. Steve's success, such a happy time for Paul Martin, left Sevrin feeling 'bittersweet – yeah, angry, proud, happy for my brothers. And jealous, lol, I wanna meet jpj [John Paul Jones] ;)'.

The years Sevrin spent growing up with his stepbrothers built a close relationship, but one strained by the move to Norway, and again by the breakdown of Steve's relationship with Sevrin 'Well I love my brothers,' Sevrin says, 'but unfortunately I only really hear from Paul. I keep in touch with Didrik's wife. I haven't heard from Henry in a while, and Elisabeth I love as well but there has been no real relationship or communication with her since they left.'

These early years were spent in what sounds like a pretty idyllic family environment. Franklin sounds rather pleasantly twee – just the suburb for a nice middle-class family to base itself. 'Today, Franklin is one of the wealthiest cities in one of the wealthiest counties in the United States,' notes the municipal website. It was founded in 1799 and named after Benjamin Franklin, and its strategic location in a crucial nexus between the American North and South made it the hugely rich centre of the plantation economy before the Civil War; but that same strategic value led to its destruction during that war, and it wasn't until the later twentieth century that it recovered that early prosperity. However, it still has a handsome nineteenth-century main street and a thriving economy drawing on agriculture, local business and bigger corporations in Nashville. It seems to be very much more picket fence than hobo.

Aside from the gig played with Slash of Guns N' Roses, described by Sevrin in the previous chapter, and hints about Albert King, we have no definite news of any big-league musical involvement on Steve's part from this period, but it seems fair to assume from that gig that he had extensive contacts among young musicians in the area, and would have taken up these opportunities whenever they arose. One of the attractions of paramedic work must have been the shift patterns, which would allow a degree of flexibility in working hours, enabling Steve to have time free to gig or record when he needed it. Perhaps the clearest conclusion of all to draw from a closer examination of Steve's career is that – despite what he has said in public about blue-collar jobs – music always came first.

SEASICK STEVE

There are interesting insights to be gained from the way in which Steve has managed the narrative of his career. His claims about a European studio seem to fit into an intriguing psychological pattern in which he is extremely defensive about any suggestion of failure, and goes to great trouble to cover his tracks. (Given his background, and the extreme self-reliance he had to develop at a very early age to survive at all, there are all kinds of plausible psychological explanations for this.) Thus, in his interview with *The Stranger*, he's glad to talk about the successes of Moon, but distracts attention from the (understandable, as far as anyone can tell) failure in Tennessee – even though by then it was it was at least ten years in the past – by pretending his last studio venture was distant both in time and geography.

Once he had made his millions as Seasick Steve, he could admit without any loss of face that the Norwegian studio was a failure. But, as we will see, in Norway there was an ongoing battle of wills between Steve and the local musicians, in which he went to great lengths to defend and define his identity. Whenever he could, he did so truthfully, but, as his situation became more desperate, he resorted to making things up – leading ultimately, perhaps, to the invention of the persona of Seasick Steve, the blues legend who convinced not only the Notodden blues community but the whole world of his backstory.

This period in Tennessee is the closest we can be sure Steve has ever lived to Mississippi. That said, even from Franklin to Como, Mississippi, just over the state border (where his friend Sherman and bluesman Mississippi Fred

McDowell lived), is a four-hour, 250-mile drive away, southwest via another crucial musical town: Memphis. The balance of probability, then, is that Steve has never actually lived in Mississippi. We don't even know for certain that he visited the state. With Elisabeth, and another three children arriving during the 1980s, not to mention a musical career to maintain, and paramedic training to complete, this period of his life must have become increasingly busy. He may have met Sherman, the buyer of wrecked guitars, at this time, probably at a musical event, although he lived far too far away for them to be more than very occasional drinking buddies.

CHAPTER 7

Olympia and Moon Music

The move to Olympia, in 1991, has been put down to Elisabeth's desire to live somewhere that looked like Norway. The story comes up in Steve's 2006 interview with bluesinlondon.com: 'Then we moved to Tennessee again, making some recordings there, but I got sick of being there so my wife said "Let's go out to Seattle." She's from Norway and I'd told her that it kinda looked like Norway there in the Northwest and she wanted to move out there.'

In his earlier, travelling days, Steve claims to have avoided Olympia, which apparently had a reputation as a violent, redneck place: He told *The Scotsman* in October 2008: 'Back in the sixties, Olympia was a redneck logging town . . . If I hitchhiked, I'd try to get a ride from Seattle to Portland and avoid Olympia 'cos it was not a nice place to get stuck in. We went there completely by accident. I had no idea that there was a punk rock thing going on.'

SEASICK STEVE

There's no evidence that Steve ever went as far north as Olympia in the sixties, other than perhaps on his West Coast pizza-parlour tour with Lightnin' Hopkins – and that wouldn't have stopped at a little place like Olympia. The second part of this statement is the more interesting bit, in some ways. Whenever the subject of their move comes up, he goes out of his way to claim that he knew nothing about grunge or riot grrrl bands at the time of the move, and that the move was just about Elisabeth wanting to see a Nordic landscape. For someone as finely tuned to the independent music scene as Steve, this is impossible to believe. It seems to be another attempt to throw us off the scent of his admirably determined musical career.

For a summary of the early history of grunge in the Northwest, see the *New York Times'* excellent feature 'Grunge: A Success Story', from November 1992. The author, Rick Marin, points out that the genre was born years before Steve appeared in the Northwest:

> In 1988, a fledgling Seattle record label called Sub Pop released a three-boxed set called *Sub Pop 200*. It was a compilation of bands like Nirvana, Soundgarden and Mudhoney, and it came complete with a 20-page booklet packed with pictures by Charles Peterson, the photographer credited with creating grunge's hair-sweat-and-guitars look. Sub Pop also sent a catalogue to the nation's alternative-rock intelligentsia describing its bands' punk-metal guitar noise as 'grunge,' the first documented use of the now-ubiquitous term. 'It could have been

sludge, grime, crud, any word like that,' said Jonathan Poneman, a Sub Pop founder.

Although Steve would probably hate the term, he fitted precisely into the category of 'the nation's alternative-rock intelligentsia'. We don't know for certain whether he received this particular booklet, but he had three years from the date the genre was given a name, until he arrived in Olympia, still claiming not to realise this was the location of a vibrant new scene. He had turned up in Nashville just as their 1980s version of new, punk-influenced music was blooming, and now he did it again in Olympia in the 1990s. In both cases he arrived a couple of years after the scene began, just as it was beginning to bloom. There was time, in both cases, for an informed observer of new music to know exactly what was going on. It's usually only the alternative-rock intelligentsia who move from new punk scene to new punk scene. The rest of the population have other priorities.

For a sense of how Steve the 1990s studio engineer understood his position on the scene, we only need look at his interview in Seattle's *The Stranger* magazine, in which he looks back on his time in the city and assesses his own place in the history of the grunge scene. He sounds much more like alternative-rock intelligentsia than he does when speaking as Seasick Steve.

'This studio has its little place in what it did here,' Wold says about the long-term impact of Moon Music in this region. 'I understand the history of it. I can see that for a period of time it was, you know,

important. I enjoyed what was going on for a while,
all the innovative bands. It was fun to record some
of the early bands.'

Steve Wold the recording engineer talks in a different way
from Seasick Steve, using longer words ('innovative') and
sentences and examining the history of the local scene in an
analytical way. Despite – sometimes – appearances, he's a
deep musical thinker.

Steve and his family probably didn't arrive in Olympia
until the summer of 1991. Sevrin was finishing middle
school and about to start high school, and Steve and
Elisabeth's oldest son, Henry James Wold, must have been
of school age too, so the move would have been timed
for the family to arrive in the summer of 1991. By this
point, many of the iconic grunge bands were already well
established, and it's difficult to believe that Steve, who
was already familiar with the new punk scene from his
time in Nashville, would not have heard of them. It seems
much more likely, therefore, that Olympia was chosen
specifically for its opportunities for an independent
recording studio. In his bluesinlondon.com interview
from 2006, Steve described his move thus:

We moved there, blind – we literally just looked
on the map and picked this town 60 miles South of
Seattle – Olympia. We show up in that town and
it turns out to be just the beginning of the punk
rock grunge thing. That's in the early 90's. So then
I brought my studio out there and set it up in the

back of a music store and started recording all these punk bands.

The first week I was there I went and saw Nirvana play, in a bar. They were great, unbelievable. I walked in and I went 'This is the shit, man!' They just wondered who the hell I was . . . I was the only old person there and I'm saying 'You guys are rockin'!' They were all suspicious of me! They had that drummer guy, the new one, Dave Grohl. Everybody in Olympia was a drummer in Nirvana for a while! Kurt (Cobain) lived upstairs from me for a while. He lived all over Olympia. People say he was from Seattle, he was from Olympia. He knew what this thing was about . . . He just was making the kind of music that he wanted to make, but I think he had a pretty good background musically.

Again, the claim that the family 'just looked on the map and picked this town' seems hard to believe. From a family point of view, there were the practicalities of schools for the children to consider. And, musically, the scene was quite well established by the time the Wolds arrived, even though Steve maintains that he didn't realise as much even in 2000, in *The Stranger*, where he says, 'I didn't really know what this music scene was . . . It was the pretty early days here. I just started doing little bands. There wasn't any real studio here.'

Nirvana is, of course, the definitive example of what was happening on the local grunge scene, and by the time Steve arrived they were on the verge of their major breakthrough.

Dave Grohl joined the band in late 1990, so by mid-1991 he could still just about be described as the new drummer. It simply seems absurd that Steve didn't know exactly who they were by this point. Their first album, *Bleach*, had come out on Sub Pop two years earlier, in June 1989, and had become a hit with exactly the kind of indie and college audience that Steve specialised in.

Nirvana had been touring nationally since that debut album was released, and in 1990 they'd signed to major label DGC records. In early 1991, they were in Sound City Studios with producer Butch Vig, recording what turned out to be the colossal breakthrough album *Nevermind*, which went on to sell 30 million copies worldwide. The success of this second album didn't just break sales records, but remoulded the expectations of independent bands, who were until Nirvana generally expected to remain with small record labels. The full extent of *Nevermind*'s success was not fully realised until the end of 1991. But an industry insider would have known they were going places years before.

As the *New York Times* reports, Sub Pop had, for all their limited resources, identified Nirvana as a good prospect: 'Nirvana's first album, *Bleach*, was recorded for $606.17 in 1989. Shrewdly, Sub Pop spent more money flying in a writer from *Melody Maker* magazine, who carried the hype back to London.'

Nor was this coverage a one-off. A glance through the back issues of the UK music press reveals more than a dozen articles featuring Nirvana in some form published in *NME*, *Melody Maker* and *Sounds* in 1989 and 1990. The tone of these pieces always made the band's breakthrough potential plain. In October 1990, for example, Keith Cameron wrote a piece in *Sounds* with the standfirst, 'If any of the US underground bands are likely to break through into the mainstream, then it's got to be NIRVANA.' The band were already a phenomenon the year before Steve rocked up 'blind' in Olympia.

Be it deliberate musical destination or random luck, however, Olympia was no longer an edgy redneck town when Steve arrived with Elisabeth, their three sons and Sevrin (who lived with them until the end of high school in 1993). Olympia had been a centre not just for logging, but all kinds of timber processing, as well as shipbuilding. In common with many British and American industrial towns, these industries declined in the 1970s, and have been to some extent replaced by the arts, services and business. Intriguingly, there's a similar history to Notodden, the Norwegian town the Wolds moved to in 2001.

The most important feature of the city's redevelopment, certainly from Steve's perspective, was the establishment in 1967 of a public liberal arts institution, Evergreen College, which had an important role in transforming the city from one with a reputation for redneck roughhousing to a beacon of progressive and feminist music. Set up specifically to offer an alternative, interdisciplinary curriculum, it boasts an impressive list of alumni, including politicians, the political activist Rachel Corrie and *The Simpsons* creator Matt Groening. Perhaps most significant, however, is the college's collection of musical students, several of whom were to work with Steve.

Besides the rapper Macklemore and rocker Conrad

Keeley, the most significant in the development of Olympia's own voice were the riot grrrl acts, including Carrie Brownstein of Sleater-Kinney, Tracey Sawyer of Heavens to Betsy and Corin Tucker who played in both (and both bands were an important part of the riot grrrl movement). However, most significant for Steve were the members of Bikini Kill, three of whom – Kathleen Hanna, Tobi Vail and Kathi Wilcox – were Evergreen alumni. Hanna was one of his studio's early customers.

One of the key Olympia groups, Beat Happening, set the Olympia tone with a series of alternative punk albums in the late 1980s. Founder Calvin Johnson was known to Steve, although the band's last LP was released in 1992, so he wouldn't have seen much of them live. Both Beat Happening and Kathleen Hanna were fans of the lo-fi aesthetic – something that clearly influenced Steve, both as recording engineer and artist. From Steve's point of view, Calvin Johnson must have been an important role model as an independent studio and label owner.

Steve set up his studio quite soon after his family arrived in the area. To bluesinlondon.com he revealed that his Olympia studio started 'in the back of a music store', and this tallies with Sevrin's recollection, that 'Between 1991 and 1994-ish . . . Moon Music was just a guitar store with a little studio in the back.' Presumably, it was helpful to be able to sell guitars (at this point with all strings included, Sevrin recalls) while building up the studio side of the business. Although Steve maintained his paramedic's qualification until 1996, Sevrin believes that he had hurt his back by this point, and could not do a job that required a lot of heavy lifting: 'Being a paramedic was before the store, but then, yes, he basically ran it all.' From now on, Steve was a full-time musician and shop and studio owner. And as far as we know, he hasn't done a non-musical job since.

From Sevrin's recollections, this sounds like one of the high points of his relationship with his father. Initially, he told me, 'I was more worried about playing sports and girls at the time.' But, as the conversation continues, it becomes clear that he looks back on his time at Moon Music the guitar shop (he'd left home by the time it became a fully fledged studio) with great affection. For a middle-aged dad, Steve was unusually cool, and only became more of a role model as the decade advanced and the studio's roster of edgy recording talent increased.

> That was pretty cool I'd have to say. Ya, I worked the counter and helped around the shop, pretty much it was just him and I working there until he hired Paul, the guitar tech. And we talked about music and he made me wanna play music because I did want to be like him. But my other parents [Victoria and Sevrin's stepfather, H Dean Sapp] did [give me] more of the encouragement to follow music. Moon recorded all sorts of cool Seattle acts like Modest Mouse, 10,000 Diving Robots, Murder City Devils, and tons more obviously.

There's no record of who Paul the guitar tech was.

Although Steve had some equipment from his Tennessee studio, he was searching for more – and of a very particular type. Sevrin says, 'When he spent time going around travelling between Washington and California looking for vintage gear, he was definitely looking for that warm vintage sound that reel-to-reel tape provided, he was kinda anti-technology at the time. Ya, I'm sure he found some on the east coast too.' Morten Gjerde, Steve's manager in Norway, with whom he lived for a while when he first arrived, remembers that 'lo-fi' was one of Steve's most important principles, one that he often mentioned when he first arrived in the country.

It would be easy to assume that the lo-fi movement was something Steve was introduced to by Calvin Johnson when he arrived in Olympia, but, if he was sourcing lo-fi equipment as soon as he arrived, he must have been a fan already. His commitment to lo-fi principles seems consistent and long-lasting. Although some writers trace the lo-fi movement back to Brian Wilson recording some early Beach Boys albums at home, the indie rock lo-fi movement is generally linked to 1980s performers such as Sebadoh and Beck. These are very much the kinds of band Steve would have followed, anyway, in his quest to find a vigorous, independent music scene. Beck also has a history performing blues, though there's nothing to connect him personally with Steve in this respect.

Despite the fact that Nashville, Olympia and Notodden in Norway, have very little in common on the face of it, there are important features about the way that music worked in all three locations that tell us something important about Steve's musical preferences. This is something that struck me first talking to Sevrin about why Steve left the States at the end of what was, by most standards, a successful decade, and one that established him as a practising musician in the way that he hadn't been in Tennessee. It's perhaps something that particularly applies to the USA – most European countries, especially countries such as Norway with well-funded arts programmes, still have some kind of noncommercial local radio that can give airtime to new or avant-garde bands.

Commenting on why Steve and Elisabeth left Olympia for Norway, Sevrin stated in an online exchange, 'I don't know why they left, dad was tired of the States or something. And I think, Same As me, He Wanted To Get To Europe Where There Is Still A Real Music scene [Sevrin's capitals].' With hindsight, though, perhaps the situation in Olympia itself has become less amenable to small-scale, independent music since Steve left. When I asked Sevrin if he still played regularly in Olympia, he replied, 'Not at all. I played there a lot in my 20s [he is now forty]. Any scene that's left is in the Seattle area. Radio here is all corporate-controlled.'

For both father and son, independent radio is crucial for a functioning indie scene. We've already seen Steve's comments about programmes such as *The X-Factor*, and we've seen that the decline of independent music radio in Nashville is one of the factors that seem to have prompted him to leave. He said a bit more about what he liked in the Olympia scene, and how it changed, in his interview with *The Stranger*:

'This period of time in the Northwest over the last 10 or 12 years has been sort of a strange island in the history of recording, because before that it was all just big record companies paying for bands to go into studios. All of a sudden, you get this so-called indie scene where people, either through little record companies or by themselves, were doing something on their own. For a while, I had great hopes for it. But so many of those indie record companies were just like miniature major companies.

'I just think it ruined it for a lot of the bands themselves,' Wold says. 'It's the same amount of work to make a record for three or four thousand dollars as it is to make a record for a hundred thousand dollars. Every time an indie label would get successful, someone would buy them. It's just all the majors gobbling each other up.'

This is undoubtedly an idealistic view of how a music scene should work, but it prevailed at Olympia for fifteen years or so, and looking at Steve's discography from those years, it's clearly true that 'this studio has its little place in what it did here'. Intriguingly, to give an instant comparison of how the local scene has changed, and to corroborate what Sevrin Johnson has said about it, *The Stranger* is now (as of 24 February 2016) reporting 'Legendary Olympia Label Struggles to Stay Afloat as Kimya Dawson and Other Artists Demand Unpaid Royalties'.

It seems that K Records, Calvin Johnson's iconic Olympia label, owes a range of its musicians substantial sums totalling many hundreds of thousands of dollars. According to some claims in the article, it has been financially mismanaged for many years. The story is complicated by that fact that other musicians also owe the label money for merchandise they have taken on tour, but the situation is summed up concisely by K Records artist Arrington de Dionyso, 'who records experimental music under his own name and heads the Indonesian-influenced garage-rock band Malaikat Dan Singa': 'The conditions in the 1990s and early 2000s that allowed an independent music scene to flourish both creatively and economically simply do not exist anymore.' The article continues:

> The decline of the culture of record buying, de Dionyso observes, has forced K to scramble to bring in enough money to pay its artists. Streaming income currently isn't making up for lost sales. He suggests that K's 'DIY Empire' could have thrived only in the 1980s and '90s, before the proliferation of streaming and illegal downloading. He allows, however, that K might not have been sufficiently savvy about the marketplace's evolving habits.

It's particularly poignant that K Records is in this predicament, because it's one of the oldest indie labels, founded in 1982, and founder Calvin Johnson has always embodied an independent, non-corporate ethos. It also makes Steve's decision to leave when he did more understandable. Although it would be overstating the case to say that Steve predicted all of this, the logical conclusion of the corporate domination he describes, when added to the power of the Internet, leads to exactly this predicament.

SEASICK STEVE

We will look at Steve's decision to leave Bronzerat Records for Warner Music in the next chapter. In many respects, when the extent of his breakthrough became clear, he seems to have decided to work by a completely different set of rules, almost to become a different person. The principles he operated by in Olympia, and in the first couple of years in Norway, no longer applied.

Before we look at the bands Steve worked with individually, there's more we can learn about him as an individual, both personally and professionally. The *Stranger* interview is the single most sensitive and insightful piece about Steve, pre- or post-breakthrough, even though even here there are odd glimpses of Steve's other agendas (for example, his misleading comments about a studio in Europe, and curious claims about not knowing the scene before he arrived).

For a quick contrast between the urbane, sensitive Steve in *The Stranger*, and what he seemed to be trying to become after his breakthrough, compare what Rick Levin says about Steve's eyes that 'shine forth with kindness, intelligence, and a sort of humoured reverence for worthwhile things', and the way Steve (now in Seasick mode) talks about his experiences of Kurt Cobain and Courtney Love in Olympia. He makes some comments of un-Steve-like bitterness and nastiness in his bluesinlondon.com interview. Published in March 2006, before his breakthrough and not long after he began performing in London, it suggests a certain grinding of gears as he changes from cerebral Steve Wold the sound engineer to Seasick Steve the punk:

He was a nice boy . . . I would have killed myself too if I was married to that chick he had [Courtney Love]! She was ugly, and she was nasty as can be man . . . We was at the Capitol Theatre [Olympia] one time and Kathleen Hanna from Bikini Kill was up on stage and Courtney walked up and hit her in the mouth! Kathleen'd told her that she had given Kurt a blow-job or something like that!

But I was sorry about him – I saw him at the airport like about a week before and I was talking to him and she come up and just took him away, right in the middle of the conversation – said 'Come on! You don't wanna be talking to him'. Then he was dead . . .

Steve seems to have fitted into the musical community in Olympia in a way he didn't, quite, in either Nashville or Norway. During the course of my research for this book, I was disappointed not to receive more contributions from the musicians Steve knew around this time. There are many – Kathleen Hanna, Calvin Johnson and Modest Mouse especially – who could have added light and shade to our understanding of Steve's character at this time. These are the musicians most widely associated with Steve, followed by a distinguished cluster of groups such as 10,000 Diving Robots and Murder City Devils, known to fans of the Northwest scene.

There is one band whose relationship with Steve we do know about, and they serve as a great example of his studio skills, described at length by Rick Levin in *The Stranger*.

SEASICK STEVE

Local trio the Tremens are described in their *Ear Pollution* interview as 'reminiscent of the tightly wound jazz-as-told-through-punk-on-a-surfboard sound of '80s seminal punksters the Minutemen', and their first full-length album, *belmont smiling racehorse downtown*, is, according to Rick Levin, 'a collection of brief but complex rock songs shot through with rapid-snap time changes, great guitar work, and a frenetic, jazzy energy'. They were the Olympia band Steve most wanted to record again. It's only fair to point out that at about the time of the *Stranger* interview Steve and the Tremens were raving about one another constantly. Although Steve doesn't disclose this in the interview, the band say they were planning to team up, with Steve as lead singer and guitarist, in an outfit called Dr Steel and the Forty-Nine's.

We know from organisers of the Notodden Blues Festival in Norway that Steve made an enquiry in May 2000 (six months before his interview with *The Stranger*) for both live touring support and album distribution for his new band, Dr Steel, before he had decided to move to Norway permanently (at which point plans for Dr Steel were shelved). So it's possible the mutual love-in was preparation for the announcement of their plans. It's also possible, of course, that Steve and the Tremens just thought of one another as fantastic. Either way, this account is the only detailed insight we have into how Steve worked as a sound engineer, and it's worth hearing on that account.

As a studio owner, Steve claims in *The Stranger* to have been persuaded to record again by the musicians themselves, having – he says – decided he was going to stop recording for the time being. He certainly never seems to have had anything as vulgar as a marketing strategy. (This low-key approach worked in Olympia, but in the more dispersed Norwegian scene was less successful.)

> 'I just got sucked in,' he says, 'and I was doing it [recording] again. You know, people started bringing bands around. Kathleen Hanna did some of the early stuff here. She brought something and Calvin [Johnson] brought Fitz of Depression.'

This was how he discovered the Tremens, as described in *The Stranger*:

> One band Wold has wanted to hear from again – and record one last time before he moves away – are the Tremens, a 'totally refreshing' Seattle trio he's been hooked on ever since he saw them play a show in Olympia years ago. 'With the Tremens,' he says, 'it was really like I heard them by accident. I just walked into this bar here in Olympia, and these guys were smokin'. I told them, 'If you guys ever want to record, I've got a studio and I'll be happy to record you.' Then they were told by other people that I wasn't just a bum.

It's immediately clear from Rick Levin's description that Steve's studio serves the music he records with a shrine-like intensity. Levin describes Steve's studio as 'an ad hoc museum dedicated to the genesis of the Olympia music scene', with an atmosphere of 'integrity, hard work, and a deep, abiding love of interesting and innovative music'. Levin observes Steve working with the Tremens closely, and his conclusions only confirm the impression he has already outlined of integrity, commitment, deep musical intelligence and sensitivity.

> In the studio, his love of the Tremens' music translates into an absolute concern with getting their sound right. His approach is both casual and entirely concentrated, unhurried yet always focused. When guitarist Quentin Ertel begins describing a particular guitar effect he has in mind, Wold sits silently, rocking back and forth in his chair, allowing him the full expression of his idea.

The Tremens work with Steve in an atmosphere of dumbstruck awe. We will read more about their work with Steve in their own interview below. Levin's conclusions at the end of a day's recording about Steve's approach to the recording process are worth recording in full, however, because they show how intimately they communed.

> The gap between the roles of producer and musician, in this instance, is virtually non-existent. It's a perfect collaboration, solidified by mutual respect and the bonds of a lasting friendship. 'There's so many things about him that I admire,' says Ertel. 'He's just a remarkable person.'
>
> From a technical standpoint, a large part of Wold's

appeal as an engineer rests in his paradoxical ability to obscure himself in the act of engaging his talents for reproduction – for lack of a better term, he serves the music. The consequences of such receptivity are made especially apparent when everyone listens back to the basic tracks, which were recorded in the space of a day, many being first takes. Even in roughest form, the songs sound amazing: clean, full, heavy, crackling with the energy of a live performance. Everyone is really happy with what's happening. Everyone smiles. At one point, Wold, stepping outside for a cigarette, tells Mitchell that 'this is the most kick-ass record that's ever come out of Moon studio'. High praise.

This is an account not just of incredible skill, but of an ability for Steve to absorb himself totally in the music, to merge his consciousness wholly into the creative process. If this is an accurate account – which it seems to be, though it's all we have – we can fully understand why Steve spent most of his life, on and off, in music studios. Bear this description in mind when we come to the failure of his Norwegian studio – he hasn't talked about much to this day, but it must have hit him very hard. Although he got a much bigger musical breakthrough than he expected or, perhaps, wanted, it wasn't on his own terms.

The Tremens seem to have disbanded some time ago. Their website – which was listed at the bottom of the interview that follows – has been deleted, and references to their music online are all more than ten years old. The crucial interview (by Craig Young) with the Tremens is buried away on earpollution.com. Although I have already referred to some sections of this in earlier chapters, it's worth reproducing more of the interview about Steve, because it's so important, and the site looks like the kind of thing that might disappear any minute.

They recorded their two albums, *belmont smiling racehorse downtown* (1999) and *Lipsicate* (2001 – one of the last things Steve recorded in Olympia), at Moon Studios, though neither disc appears on the Moon Studios discographies page. The only record I have been able to trace online is their now very obsolete MySpace page. There was obviously a very warm relationship between Steve and the band (guitarist Quentin Ertel, bassist John Mitchell and drummer Curtis Andreen). The band eulogise his abilities both as a recording engineer and producer and as a guitarist and singer. After Craig Young, the interviewer, has raised the topic of their work with 'Northwest icon' Steve, the band describe their meeting and the close relationship they all quickly built, and they get down to musical business:

> *So he's the fifth Beatle – or the fourth Tremen, as the case would be.*
> **Quentin:** He never goes out to shows . . . ever, and for some reason he came out that night [when they first met at a Tremens gig]. We then went and did our first record with him [*belmont smiling racehorse downtown*] and he then asked us to be his backup band. So we actually cut a record with him that never came out.

Really. What kind of music is it?

Curtis: We were called Dr Steel and the Forty-Nine's.

Quentin: It sounded kinda like ZZ Top with a delta feel to it. Lots of slide.

Mitchell: That guy is . . .

Curtis: He's a fucking *awesome* guitar player!

Mitchell: . . . unbelievable!

Quentin: And his voice . . .

Mitchell: Sounds like Joe Cocker.

Curtis: We were going to go on tour with him, then he found out there was this huge blues scene in Norway and ended up moving there

Yeah, I've heard that, too.

Curtis: It's a great stepping stone for him. He's got all this old recording equipment that no one has over there, much less has ever seen.

Quentin: One of the big things Steve has done for us and this band is simply to be able to know and interact with someone with his kind of history and his kind of accomplishments under his belt. I'm not just talking about the records he's recorded here in the Northwest that have gone on to be really influential, I'm also talking about the bands that he's played with over the years.

Who has he played with?

Mitchell: Everyone from the Beach Boys to . . . Who was that band he first played with?

Quentin: Shanti.

Mitchell: Shanti, who also included Aashish Khan,

and Ravi Shankar's tabla player, Zakir Hussain. They were one of the first bands to intertwine East Indian music with rock.

Hussain's tabla playing is incredible!

Mitchell: Steve knows all those people . . . he knows *everybody*. And he's got stories you wouldn't believe. Everything from hitchhiking and getting picked up by Jimi Hendrix, to playing with people like Albert King and a ton of other blues guys. But the coolest thing about him is his attitude, which is simply 'God forgive the soul who wants to be a rock star.'

It was a cool marriage between us because if we had somebody else, some Northwest producer – and there are many of them who are dialed into whatever scene and carry a lot of weight in those scenes – it would have not been the same. With Steve there was no weight to be carried, there was no scene to be talked up, there was nothing but some people who got along and wanted to make music that's different from all the other stuff out there.

Quentin: In our eyes he's got integrity for miles. And for him to think highly of our band is perhaps the single biggest compliment we could ever receive.

Many of Seasick Steve's fans wonder why it took him so long to begin performing. We now know that he was planning to start a band from about 1999, and continued determinedly with (different) performing plans once he arrived in Norway. When he arrived in Norway, according to his then manager Morten Gjerde, he had a demo CD, called *Dr Steel*. He didn't say much to Gjerde about this, and all Gjerde has told me is that it's 'very funky music'. Unfortunately, it has never been released.

Otherwise, the band's comments are worth seeing in their entirety to get a cumulative impression of how awestruck they were by working with Steve. This interview is not dated, but it sounds as though they have already accepted that Dr Steel wouldn't go ahead, so they're not just promoting themselves.

Aside from the Tremens' adulation of Steve, the discography of Moon Music is a spare document, with none of the human interest of this interview. And it's not even a complete and fully accurate document. When Rick Levin asks Steve for an estimate of the number of albums Steve has recorded, Steve says, 'Must be like 30 or 40 or 50, a lot of albums. Maybe more than that. I don't know what happens to a lot of them. It's hard to keep track. People come, make a record, and I never hear from them again.' For starters, neither of the Tremens' albums is on the studio's discogs page. Steve's business wouldn't, of course, all have been albums for release: there would have been plenty of work recording demos, vanity projects and commercial projects too, if he had wanted it.

The earliest Moon album to be released, which must have been recorded as soon as the studio moved out of the guitar shop, is *PEZ*, from 1994, which Levin describes as 'a recording of a band Wold and Paul [Schuster] put together called Pez, the record coming out on London's Rough Trade label'. One of only a few of the bands Steve recorded who are still on the road are The Emerald

SEASICK STEVE

Down (often referred to as TED), founded in 1995 and then consisting of Rebecca Basye (guitar and vocals), Joel Schumacher (drums) and Jessica Marshall (bass and vocals). The band's current label, Saint Marie Records, has this description on its website:

> Yes, in typical Pacific Northwest style it was indeed named after the race track that opened its doors at the same time. However, not so typical for the PNW at the time was TED's huge, effects-driven wall of sound laced with harmonious vocals. One of only a few Pacific Northwest – indeed American – bands in the genre at the time whose contemporaries were largely located in the UK, they were a lone reed amongst a sea of mostly low-fi regional scenesters fairly unfamiliar with or adapted to TED's genre.

The band were mostly inactive in 2003–15, but now, after several personnel changes, are back on the road. Their style is rather different from Steve's typical Olympia customers, and shows that he was open to anything with some independent spirit about it. This is Saint Marie's summary of Moon and that period of the band's career:

> By their second year [1996] TED recorded a four song, self-titled EP with engineer Scott Swayze at Steve Wold's Moon Studios in Olympia. In the early days TED thinks it remembers playing a number of shows with the likes of Unwound, Karp, Beck, Heavenly, Hovercraft and King Black Acid in the

Pacific Northwest US, and was voted as among the top 25 PNW bands by Seattle's *Pandemonium* magazine.

Also released in 1996 were the hardcore punk outfit Fitz of Depressions' final album *Swing*, which was released on Calvin Johnson's K Records, and is one of several projects Johnson brought to Moon Studios – even though he did, of course, have his own studio. Similar are the Third Sex, whose album *Card Carryin'*, recorded and mixed by Steve and produced by Donna Dresch, appeared the same year. Behead the Prophet NLSL [No Lord Shall Live] also released their only album, *I Am That Great And Fiery Force*, that year. It was described by AllMusic as 'pure noise that's barely kept in beat while "singer" Joshua Plague spouts off at the top of his lungs', and it's hard to know how rewarding Steve found some of these; but years of listening to the more regular punk might have fed into his own sound. It would be fascinating to hear his view.

On the face of it, indie rockers 764-Hero, who released both a single and their album *Salt Sinks and Sugar Floats* in 1996, might be more Steve's cup of tea. They collaborated frequently with Modest Mouse over the following few years, but AllMusic doesn't reckon the stardust rubbed off:

From the opening snare of 'Impossible Waste', it becomes obvious that 764-HERO isn't exactly about originality. And the rest of the album doesn't do anything to disprove that claim, instead cementing it as fact. 764-HERO's music just isn't groundbreaking by anyone's standards – they just sound like a conglomeration of all the various Northwest area bands of the '90s.

Bangs, a trio of Sarah Utter, Jesse Fox and Maggie Vail (sister of Tobi Vail from Bikini Kill), were on the fringes of the riot grrrl movement, though they identified themselves more with a straightforward rock sound, which they provide on this album with brio. They released a single in 1999, and their album *Sweet Revenge* the following year, both recorded at Moon Studios.

Kathleen Hanna, meanwhile, is harder to trace officially. Steve told Rick Levin that 'Kathleen Hannah [*sic*] did some of the early stuff here', and also told *The Arts Desk*, in June 2011:

> Kathleen Hanna was the first person I recorded at my studio. I liked her but she was a teenager, maybe 20, and I was old. They were suspicious of me at first. I had no idea about punk and what they were doing. Then all these girl bands came, dyke bands. They'd look at me like some redneck guy but I don't have much of a deal about any of that so after about five minutes it was OK and I became the favourite girl-band studio.

There is no reason to lie about something like this. The projects Hanna and the other riot grrrl bands brought could perfectly well have been demos or private projects. Hanna (as a solo artist) was so lo-fi for much of the nineties that projects such as *Julie Ruin* (1998) were recorded in her apartment, and she didn't use studios.

Of course, the big recording deal for Moon Studios was Modest Mouse, who recorded the album *This Is a Long Drive for Someone With Nothing to Think About* (1995), the EP *Interstate 8* (1996), the album *The Lonesome Crowded West* (1997) and, for many fans, the revelatory compilation of singles and rarities (some but not all of which were recorded at Moon Studios) *Building Nothing Out of Something* (1999). As Brent DiCrescenzo's *Pitchfork* review of the last of these notes, 'The roar of punk splashes against the melancholy of roots music', which could – of course – also be said of Seasick Steve. Of all of the bands Steve recorded, Modest Mouse matches his own stylistic interests and tendencies best.

Modest Mouse didn't become platinum-selling stars until *Good News for People Who Love Bad News*, released in 2004, as Seasick Steve was just beginning to make a name for himself in the 12 Bar Club in Soho. But, by the time they recorded the acclaimed *The Moon & Antarctica* (2000), released on the major label Epic Records, they had probably outgrown Moon Studios, so even if he had stayed in Olympia, it's unlikely he would have recorded much more Modest Mouse. As usual, far from being lucky, Steve has shown himself to be a shrewd reader of the ebb and flow of the musical scene, and, as he says, more or less, to Rick Levin, he could tell that the indie scene in Olympia was slowly running out of steam.

Steve must have known he was recording something quite special, however: right from those two early albums recorded at Moon Studios, they were picked up by discerning listeners, and critics with an eye for intriguing sounds or just the next coolest thing. Isaac Brock's guitar playing is central to the band's unmistakable, idiosyncratic sound, as Brian Howe describes very well in his *Pitchfork* review of the 2014 reissue:

> But it's the guitars that really define it, so strange and particular – Brock's hearty riffs, string bends, harmonics, and whammy-bar tremolo push up toward trebly extremes of panicked intensity. The songs break down into wheezes and coughs as the band pounds the ends of bars until they curl up like sheet metal.

His lyric-writing is also highly original, and, as Howe says, deeply rooted in the psycho-geography of provincial America.

> His lyrics are marked by a war between militant atheism and kind of crypto-Christian mysticism, a tension that twists his perspective into strange shapes. On these records, the pavement is steadily encroaching on the wild in ways that feel spiritually symbolic. Brock wants to wrench apart ground and sky, prefabricated towns and consumer culture, to find an exit hatch into some deeper, more meaningful state of being which, as he suspects on 'Exit Does Not Exist', is a fantasy.

Steve has quite a few credits on their songs for guitar, slide guitar or similar, and went on tour with Modest Mouse as backing guitarist, as Levin confirms. The dates are hard to pin down, but it was probably 1995, when they were touring their first album. Steve's musical role with the band is only really a continuation of the kind of playing he's been doing, on and off, since 1960s San Francisco.

The contentment of Steve's life in Olympia radiates from the pages of *The Stranger*. It seems to have given him everything he wanted from music: fairly regular playing, lots of studio work, a respected place on an independent scene and a relatively low profile. He seems to have thought he was getting more of the same in Notodden. It didn't quite work out the way he expected, but then he created a performing persona that projected him into celebrity orbit, and the rest is history.

By the time he left Olympia, then, he had firm touring and recording plans for Dr Steel, his band with the Tremens. Why had he left it until the age of fifty to write his own music and lead his own band, given his major-label debut was at the age of twenty? We can only suggest educated guesses about this, but it was probably partly a question of finding backing-guitar work harder to come by for a middle-aged man. He may have been waiting until he had some financial security and could afford the time away from recording. Perhaps it was also a matter of needing time to develop his own musical ideas – which he could filter through the fascinating experience of recording so much great music at Moon Studios.

It was also, I would suggest, a question of confidence.

SEASICK STEVE

Seasick Steve may not come across as a personality lacking in self-confidence – but, then, the character Seasick Steve seems to be is, to some extent, a disguise and an escape. Because of his aggressive stepfather and isolated childhood, and to some extent the decades of false starts his musical career suffered, it seems that Steve did lack confidence about performing in public. He seems to have been more comfortable in small groups of people he knew well and trusted, from the members of Shanti to the Tremens. Perhaps it took six years of being fêted as an 'icon' of the Northwest scene to build his confidence to the point of leading his own band. If so, he needed all the confidence he could muster for the rollercoaster ride to come.

CHAPTER 8

Norway

We know more about the years 2000 and 2001 than entire decades earlier in Steve's life. The picture painted is of agonising decisions balancing family against career, and performance against recording. On the face of it, it can't really be said to have worked: the vintage studio Steve so eagerly brought to what seemed to be an active and receptive blues scene was sold on at a knockdown price, for the Norwegian musical community to use. Steve and his family went on to spend most of their time in Cornwall – he didn't really seem to have settled comfortably in Notodden. However, the crisis Steve was plunged into by the failure of the studio, the disintegration of the his band the Level Devils and his heart attack seems to have provoked one of the most astonishing bursts of creative rebirth in recent musical history, as he recorded his breakthrough album,

Dog House Music, in his kitchen, alone save for occasional help from his sons.

It all started with a road trip that Steve and Elisabeth took around Norway in May 2000. According to a report published in August 2001 in the Norwegian national tabloid *Dagbladet*, the couple were actually looking for somewhere to retire to. It wasn't originally Notodden that they were considering, but Ålesund, a much larger and very picturesque town on the west coast of Norway. The article's standfirst is, '"The family should be settled in Ålesund and I should be retired. Instead I packed my studio into a container and went to Notodden. The city's blues enthusiasm caught me," says Steve Wold.'

This is confirmed by another report in local newspaper *Telen*, from March 2001, stating that the decision to move to Notodden was made 'during a road trip in Norway with [Steve's] Norwegian wife Elisabeth in May last year'. This is the same report that told us the decision was influenced not by the blues festival but by Elisabeth's love of Dag Solstad's *T. Singer*.

Retirement wasn't the only thing on Steve's mind, however. Music was still niggling away at him, as it always has. It seems he was still trying to plan a tour for the band he had created with the Tremens, and a distributor for their album. And if he was planning to tour with that band, was he really thinking of retiring to Norway, just at the point that he was trying to launch a band, with three-quarters living in Olympia?

Espen Fjelle, currently director of the Blues Senter in Notodden (which now includes the Juke Joint Studio) and active as both musician and organiser on the local scene for decades, told me in an email, 'When Steve approached Notodden for the very first time (in May 2000) he tried to book his band at that time, Dr Steel, to tour Europe in the fall. The band had just released an album, and Steve was seeking both a European/Norwegian booking agency and a distribution company for the album.'

It seems that they all got chatting, and Steve got the hard sell from the Norwegian musical community. The same *Dagbladet* article quotes him as saying, 'I mentioned that I had a studio, and thus it was done. "Take it here!" came the cry, and now it has arrived. We just packed it up. I've had it for years, but was going to sell it before we moved to Norway.'

This may have been a sudden change of plan – a last chance to run a profitable studio in a busy blues scene – because it sounds very much as though the studio was originally due to be sold to provide a retirement nest egg for Steve before leaving the USA, and that life in Norway was to represent retirement with some performing on the side. The *Dagbladet* article goes on: 'And he was offered 1.7 million for equipment, reveals Morten Gjerde, former festival director and now Wold's assistant in the reconstruction of The Juke Joint Studio.' At today's exchange rate, 1.7 million Norwegian Kroner is about $200,000, or £140,000. So, probably enough to provide a modest retirement. Bear the value of the studio in mind, too, because it's much more than Steve eventually sold it for.

The plot thickens slightly when we discover (again in *Dagbladet*) that, 'He heard about the record company Blue

SEASICK STEVE

Town Records' [*sic*] dream of building up a proper studio'. Bluestown Records was founded in 2000 by Morten Gjerde, Jostein Forsberg, Øyvind Sauarlia and two others who have subsequently sold their shares. The label releases albums by most of the prominent local blues musicians, and a few outsiders, mostly those who perform at the festival. This is the same company that Steve refused to release *Cheap* with. It would clearly be very helpful for the label to have its own studio, and to all intents and purposes, it does. The Juke Joint Studio – what was Steve's studio – is not now owned by Bluestown Records, but as part of the Blues Senter in Notodden is a valuable communal resource, and it is an associate partner of the record company.

Initially, Steve seems to have realised a slightly greater valuation for his share of studio when it was set up in Norway than he would to have sold in the USA. *Dagbladet* reported, 'Yesterday morning [1 August 2001], they signed with the landlord of the premises after the building process was well underway. Notodden AS [essentially the local council] has allocated 150,000 kroner to the project, and the guys have applied for 550,000 kroner from SND [a regional development body]. Steve Wold's equity in the project is 1.9 million.' So, when the contract with the landlord of the premises was signed, Steve's share was valued at 1.9 million kroner, in a total valuation of 2.6 million, representing 73 per cent ownership.

We will look at how this unravelled in due course, though Steve was to sell off portions of this concern until the last part was sold for a pittance. I have only the Norwegians' version of this story. In the end, they got the studio they wanted. They had persuaded Steve to bring his to Notodden; he didn't get enough business to make it viable, so they bought it from him for a knockdown price. They now have a glorious vintage studio. From a purely business angle, Steve would almost certainly have made more money selling up in Olympia. Until and unless Steve speaks up himself, that is as much as we will know.

So there appears to be an intriguing cluster of overlapping reasons given for the Wold family's move to Norway, and an unusual amount of detail, in a life delineated so far by scraps of information. There is no reason they couldn't all be true, at least partially. Musically, there was the attraction of a big blues scene in Notodden. We can now provide a likely date – May 2000 – for the point at which Steve discovered, as the Tremens remarked in their interview with earpollution.com, that Norway had a sizeable blues scene. We've already looked at Steve's ambivalence about the blues scene – an ambivalence that seems, like his views on so much, to change some time in 2003. Anyway, at the time he was looking to move, the local interest in blues music obviously provided an attraction. He also remarked on this to *Telen*, as we saw in Chapter 2.

Steve's son Sevrin sums all of the reasons succinctly in our online exchange: 'Dad was tired of the States or something. And I think, Same As me, He Wanted To Get To Europe Where There Is Still A Real Music scene [Sevrin's capitals].' The only comment Steve has made that might indicate he was indeed fed up with living in the USA is this remark in *The Stranger*: '"This is it," says Wold about his reasons for leaving. "I'm finished with

America. I'm 50 years old now, and I've been watching greed play the main stage since I was a teenager. I just can't stand it anymore."'

If that is how he felt about the Democratic 1990s, his departure was well timed to avoid George W Bush. The US presidential election of 2000, between George W Bush and Al Gore, took place on 7 November, almost exactly the time Steve visited Notodden to look for houses and studio locations. Bush became president on 20 January 2001, and Steve and family were out of the country by June that year.

Finally, Elisabeth must have made some contribution to this decision. After thirty years in America, it's quite likely that she wanted to return to Norway for more personal reasons than purely an affection for the novels of Dag Solstad. Although no one has said so on the record, it's easy to imagine her yearning for a quiet life in Ålesund, a centre of genteel senescence – rather like a kind of Nordic Bognor Regis. We can't be sure about her motivation, of course, but we can be sure that, if she wanted a quiet life in Norway, she must have been disappointed.

Although it is less beautiful than Ålesund, there is no doubt that Notodden has both beauty and cultural magnetism, unusual for such a small place. In *Dagbladet* Steve observed,

'Notodden was dead when its industry closed down. And then enthusiasts gave the city new life with a major focus on blues culture. I've never been involved in anything like it. In the United States this miracle has never happened!' Blues was the reason

that it was Notodden and not Ålesund, as the Wold
family originally intended.

This last comment is not really true, since it also applies
to some extent to Olympia, which changed from a tough
logging town to somewhere with a distinguished and
vibrant cultural scene. A little flattery does no harm when
you are opening a studio in an unfamiliar town, of course.

Like Olympia, Notodden is a former industrial town
reinvented by the arts and education, though much
smaller, with a population of about 9,000, as opposed
to Olympia's citizenship of nearly 50,000. Some seventy
miles southwest of Oslo, the town is strategically located
on an important waterway and near waterfalls that have
been used for hydropower generation. The electricity
generated was used in iron foundries and fertiliser
factories, and between them these industries dominated
the town. When they declined in the 1980s as the works
relocated elsewhere, there was a gradual diversification
into hi-tech industry and services.

Notodden's early industrial development (technically,
the 'Rjukan-Notodden Industrial Heritage Site') was
included on the UNESCO World Heritage list in 2015 both
for its historic value and beautiful natural location. This
heritage, along with an abundance of disused industrial
buildings looking for a new creative home, has made
Notodden a perfect location for cultural events.

Blues music has featured on the local scene for many
years. The town's blues festival started in 1988, and today
is one of the largest events of its kind in Europe. It attracts

about 30,000 visitors a year, with starry international headliners as well as extensive stage opportunities for local artists such as the Notodden Blues Band, who've been active since the mid-1970s. We can already see why this might provide an appealing proposition for Steve and his studio, ready for a new challenge and sick of Bush's America. Oil-rich Norway is famous for its generous patronage of the arts. This certainly isn't a place where, as Steve described America, 'greed play[s] the main stage'. And there's both an active local scene, and, with the festival, a keen international profile among blues musicians. On paper, then, it had everything. Steve could have written a great business plan to move the studio to Notodden.

Surprisingly, Steve's life in Norway is one of the most fully documented periods of all. I have had some very valuable insight into his first few years in Notodden from Morten Gjerde, who is a Norwegian documentary photographer with extensive involvement in the city's blues scene, including four years on the board of Notodden Blues Festival (1996–2000), with the last two as director – and, as one of the founders of Bluestown Records.

Most importantly, though, he was Steve's manager from the moment he arrived in Norway to the recording of *Cheap*. Plus, as we've already seen, Steve was sufficiently exotic to entice local newspaper *Telen* into regular reports about his goings-on, which offer a fascinating chronicle of gradually shifting characters and relationships. In the beginning, in November 2000, and for at least eighteen months afterwards, Steve was effusing warmth about his new home like a Scandinavian log fire in the depths of winter. He really seems to have been charmed by the Norwegians on his first visit in May 2000, and there is a strong sense from the detailed accounts of his arrival in the local press that he was engaged in a determined charm offensive. Witness the start to an article, entitled 'Things Take Time', published in *Telen* on 10 July 2001: 'Steve Wold visited Notodden last summer. He enjoyed himself so much that he decided to settle in the city.' It is illustrated with a cheery photo of Steve with Morten Gjerde, presumably in Morten's home. Steve then returned on his own in November 2000 to begin to make practical arrangements for home and studio, and *Telen* caught up with him again. We've already read the second part of that report, in which Steve effuses about his musical youth; in the first, he is full of praise for his new hometown:

> Wold, who currently lives in Seattle with his family, fell completely, not only for the city but also for the people who live here: 'In addition to searching for a suitable property, I have met so many positive and enthusiastic people here in town. It is absolutely amazing there are so many people who are doing music in a such a small town.'

Even at this early stage of the move, Steve made sure to make contact with the most important musical figures locally, in what reads like a strategically planned attempt to establish his new studio in the heart of the local blues scene: 'He had time to practise with R&B Express, he visited Kåre Virud and jammed with him and Jostein Forsberg in

Skien, he has been on the blue team, met with Notodden Development with a view to establishing his lo-fi studio.'

These figures are the most important on the local scene: Kåre Virud is the Norwegian translator of Dylan and a crucial founding figure on the Notodden blues scene in the 1970s, helping to establish a local blues scene sung in the Norwegian language. Jostein Forsberg is now CEO of the Notodden Blues Festival and has been involved in running it for many years. He is also an elected member of the Memphis-based organisation the Blues Foundation. And Notodden Development is a local agency that provided funding for the building and setup costs. While Steve's desire to make contact with the key local figures is entirely understandable, and in many ways just good business practice, the fact that he chose to move to a scene that, unlike Olympia, is so exclusively dominated by blues music suggests that – despite his later denials – he must have found the genre at least bearable at this stage.

A separate report from March 2001, illustrated by a businesslike photo of Steve and his carpenter – one Vegard Finnekåsa – in the still-unconverted warehouse building that would soon become Juke Joint Studio, confirms the municipal financial arrangement, and Steve's own career plans:

Notodden AS has supported him financially to build the studio, which he hopes and believes will eventually be used widely by both Norwegian as well as European musicians and bands. He hopes to make this a full-time job in the long term, as it has been at home in the US. There are many musicians

and bands that deeply regret that he is packing up
and leaving them for good.

The July report continues with great detail about the
building plans and timescale, including the arrival of
the container with Steve's studio equipment, later in the
week that the article was published. It then confirmed that
a special acoustic construction would house the studio,
which was due to open in time for the 2001 Notodden
Blues Festival in early August 2001: '"A 'box' for musicians
during recording is being built,' said Steve. It's less than a
month to the blues festival and there is great PR value in
having the studio ready so people can see it then."'

Steve made a point of emphasising the quality, rarity and
specialism of his studio equipment at every opportunity.
As the Tremens remarked, he believed that having high-
quality vintage gear, some of it from the famous STAX
studios, would be a selling point, and made sure he said so
as often as possible. The March *Telen* article observed:

People have said that when you go into Steve's
studio it's like going into a studio from the 1960s.
Steve has long collected old tube-driven studio
equipment, and among the treasures found an are
old mixing desk from the legendary STAX studio in
Memphis, which produced many best-sellers in the
Sixties with a unbelievable sound.

And in July, just to make sure the information remained
fresh: 'With him from Seattle in the US, he has a complete

recording studio, with equipment from including Stax Studios. But when can construction start?' Fortunately, everything was finished on time. Morten Gjerde confirms that, 'The studio equipment was set up and everything was ready for an opening session on 5 August 2001, as part of the Notodden Blues Festival 2001.'

Several of the early newspaper reports talk about the difficulty of finding suitable accommodation, and, during Steve's early visits in November 2000 and March 2001, he stayed with Morten Gjerde. He seems to have found a family house by August 2001. In keeping with everything else about Steve, it was in the vintage style, and needed some maintenance and cosmetic repair. In August 2001 *Dagbladet* reported, 'Now Steve, his wife Elisabeth (originally an Oslo girl) and their sons of 12, 14 and 17 are installed in an old villa. It will be restored to its original condition and in good retro style he is hunting for a sink, wood-burning stove and pretty, old kitchen.' To which Steve adds, '"It must be done quickly, otherwise my wife will kill me. I've already thrown out the kitchen."'

There is no report from anyone about the success of the studio opening, but it wasn't long until Steve was itching to take up where he left off with the Tremens and their album *Dr Steel and the Forty-Nine's* in Olympia, and start performing as a musician. We've already seen how keen Steve was to make something of Dr Steel and the Forty-Nine's, his band with the Tremens, and it wasn't just Espen Fjelle he approached. He told Morten Gjerde about it when he stayed with him in 2000, while looking around

Notodden for places to live and locate his studio before his move. Morten wrote to me:

> It was one of the first things he brought over to my house, and that was before he moved to Norway . . . Dr Steel was a band with young locals from Olympia, WA, that Steve recorded an album with. I think it was just a recording project, but maybe Steve wanted to make some more out of it if could he find a way for it, and when he got in touch with Notodden he maybe hoped this could be the breakthrough for the project? I don't know – but Steve gave me the CD and just say it was some young musicians that he made a session with in Moon Studios. Very funky music by the way :)

From what Espen Fjelle said about Steve's request for a distributor and a booking agent for Dr Steel, it seems that, in May 2000, he was planning both a live and recording career for his band with the Tremens. (Was he really planning to retire? Is that a story he told Elisabeth to justify a move to a place with an active music scene? Or one he told *Dagbladet*, to disguise the seriousness of his musical ambition?) By the time his move to Norway was complete, the following year, those plans must have been shelved as being impractical – the band leader and backers were thousands of miles apart. There is some uncertainty in the report from Morten Gjerde about the timing of Steve's next move into performance, but, looked at afresh, it seems pretty clear that Steve was determined to forge a career as a performer.

SEASICK STEVE

Morten Gjerde told me, 'Anyway, from the time of his move and for the first year or so, he was just into studio work as sound engineer, sometimes with a producer title. He had no plans for bands or artist sessions at that moment, but after a time, and when he see that he not had too much income . . . he decided to start a side project as a musician. Then we built Seasick Steve and the Level Devils.'

It's interesting to hear that a lack of income from the studio was affecting Steve's decisions so early on. At the same time, Gjerde may be underestimating Steve's determination to perform. The timing he outlines above does not fit with his own chronology, explained below, about the beginning of his career as Seasick Steve – which seems to have first shown signs of life only a month or two after the Juke Joint Studio opened:

It was around September 2001 that Steve wanted to put together a band and start to play acts as a musician. So far, he had been in the studio, as engineer and producer. It was then my task to introduce Steve to potential musicians. A common friend of ours had a childhood friend who played drums and who had just returned from an extended stay in London. Kai Kristoffersen was the person that was chosen as the drummer.

Then I brought Steve to Oslo, where I introduced him to an old friend, Jan-Olov Husmo (Mr Jo) as a bass player. At home in Jan-Olov's living room, Steve played through a series of songs he had written recently and Mr Jo play accompanied him on upright bass, like a jam session, and after an hour it was clear that we had a match and a new trio. Steve, Kai and Jan-Olov. Seasick Steve & The Level Devils was born. The date of the meeting in Jan Olov's house in Oslo was 29 September 2001. The whole meeting, conversation and playing was recorded by me and are today in my private collection.

So, within two months of opening his Juke Joint Studio in Notodden, Steve had also set off on the musical career that was, after five years' graft, to bring him such incredible success. Given what we know about his plans for Dr Steel, before he moved to Norway, it seems very clear that at this point Steve was determined to begin performing. From what others (Morten Gjerde and the Tremens) have said about the music on the Dr Steel album, it doesn't sound so very different from Seasick Steve's – a kind of funky, rootsy nu-blues. And in December 2001, Steve gave what must be the first public performance of some of his new material at a local Christmas blues gig. Inevitably, Knut H Slettemo from *Telen* was on hand to report (published 10 December 2001):

> Friday was finished off at the Bellman Pub, where Notodden House Rockers ensured swinging blues into the night. This was the first time Notodden experienced studio owner Steve Wold as a singer and guitarist. The band performed several of his own songs, to the delight of an audience that consisted of several visiting blues weekend guests.

SEASICK STEVE

The only mystery is why Morten Gjerde should say that Steve started performing in Norway because of a lack of income at the studio, when there surely wasn't time – in six weeks – to determine what sort of a living Juke Joint Studio would provide. In fact, the studio seems to have got off to a decent start, and there is no indication until late 2003 – well after Seasick Steve and the Level Devils were up and running, and the disagreements over the band's record label had already taken place – that Steve was concerned about the lack of income. In December 2001, four months after the studio opened, *Telen* was on hand again to publish a feature about a young local band, Up to Fly, who were using the studio. Unless Steve is not being truthful here (and there was no reason for him to lie), all was well at this stage:

> Steve Wold has finally got everything in place in their new premises. It has taken time to rig up the old studio that he took with him from the United States. 'I'm very pleased so far,' said Steve. Adding that this applies to the reception he has received in Notodden, his position in the industrial park and the interest to use his studio.

The band, too, seemed to have understood the studio's particular advantages:

> 'We chose this studio because it is analogue. It means that everything we play is going onto the album. In a digital studio the sound can be fixed afterwards.

It's going well here,' said an enthusiastic John Olav
Hovde, the guitarist of the band.

It's possible that Morten Gjerde was conflating several
different events in what he told me, nearly fifteen years
after the events. While a lack of income from the studio
may have affected Steve's mood and musical outlook from
2003 onwards, and influenced the dark mood of *Dog House
Music*, it cannot possibly have had any effect on *Cheap*,
much of which was written and recorded within months
of the studio's opening. Local musical politics are murky
and impossible to decipher completely with access to only
one side of the story, and many years down the line. We've
seen, however, that Bluestown Records wanted its own
studio. It wouldn't have been a disaster for the Norwegian
musical community to take control of Juke Joint Studio
themselves, which is roughly the situation today. It is 67
per cent owned by local musician Espen Fjelle, but also part
of the town's Blues Senter, and used in collaboration with
Blues Festival events.

Morten Gjerde has, however, been very helpful with
other details about Steve's life at this point. He was
present, and witnessed at first hand the creation of the
performing name 'Seasick Steve'. Since it took place
when Steve was still living with him, it must have been
on one of the musician's earlier visits to Notodden, either
November 2000 or March 2001:

During the period he lived with us, I worked as
a manager for a local band and we were going to

Denmark on tour. I asked if Steve would join us, but he was reluctant because of the boat ride between Norway and Denmark. He joined after some persuasion. On the way to the ferry, I told a story about a little difficult meeting I had had a few years earlier with the American blues legend 'Homesick James' in Oslo. After this story was finished, I just said, without any thought, that [whereas] he called himself Homesick James, you can take the name Seasick Steve. There was some laughter, and later on when Steve was being seasick on the boat, the name was really established. When he chose to put together a band a couple of years later, it was his own choice that his artist's name would be Seasick Steve.

In fact, if Steve called himself 'Seasick Steve' from his first meeting with bassist Jan-Olov on 29 September 2001, it would have been less than a year between the creation of the name and the startup of the band.

After this, the details of the band's internal relations become a little confused. Gjerde says, 'I worked as a manager/tour-manager from the beginning until November 2002' – so, for just over a year. It was a crucial and productive year, however, as we'll see. 'When I quit, Mr Jo [Husmo] took over most of my job, and after a time the drummer Kai Kristoffersen also quit the band,' he explained. 'Mr Jo then opened a door for Dan Magnusson, who was the drummer in Jan-Olov's Swedish band Harry Banks Buzzers. Dan (nicknamed Papa-Dan) lives in Åmål, Sweden and is still playing as Steve's regular drummer.'

There's little sense from Gjerde of why the band's personnel changed so rapidly, or why he himself left. He did promise, when I first got in touch, not to reveal any details of personal disagreements with Steve, so it can probably be assumed that the reason lies in some sort of personality clash. It cannot have been for a lack of productivity, because, for a new group who had never met one another before, they got down to business extremely effectively. Steve, in particular, seems to have been brimming with ideas. The situation becomes clearer when we look at Morten Gjerde's invaluable account of how the band's first album, *Cheap*, came about:

> Around the time of summer/autumn 2002, a demo CD for use in promotional work was produced. This included songs from the repertoire that Steve presented for Jan-Olov in Oslo at their first meeting. Steve had written the songs between the time he stayed with me [late 2000] and 2002. Steve had new songs in his head all the time. Initially, they took the form of more funky riffs than the expression that later become as his trademark.
>
> The first demo by Seasick Steve, which came in the autumn of 2002, has many of the same songs as the *Cheap* album. This was titled: *Sick of Slick – Lo-Fi*. The last reference to a concept Steve enjoyed using that genre designation for his music, lo-fi blues. This was burned in his own CD burner, but had designer produced booklet that was professionally pressed and private printed label to mount on the CD-R plate.

Cheap came first like a homemade demo (DSR0035) in a white cardboard envelope with a factory-pressed CD disc. Where all the hallmarks that are outside cover art of *Cheap* copied on a home-office copy-machine, then cut and pasted on the envelope by hand. I do not know for sure how many copies were made, but I'm guessing about a hundred.

This was released with a kind of 'proxy label' – There's A Dead Skunk Records. This company didn't exist as a registered company at that time, but was made by Steve for personal reasons. He would not release the album on the local record company Bluestown Records [sic], and to show everybody else that he had got a record deal, he established a label with an as yet unregistered address in Clarksdale, Mississippi. The plan was that Steve and Jan-Olov should have this company together in the future. I recognise that Steve uses this company today, and as such the company is certainly now more tangibly established as a corporation.

So after this first handcrafted version, a new edition was printed. Still limited edition and the same catalog number (DSR0035), but this time in a digi-pack version with inlaid booklet. This version has also, like the first one, thirteen songs.

Later [*Cheap* was released by Bronzerat in 2007] Bronzerat pressed the first version that is publicly available and in regular circulation (BR05). This was also a digi-pack version, but without booklet and without the 'Limited Edition' and with only twelve songs. One song was removed (track nine, 'Walkin' with the Devil'). The song was later referred to as 'the lost track' by the fans. This song was taken away by Steve because it had a guest musician who played harmonica and Steve found out for personal reasons that he would not credit him in the cover, so when the album *Cheap* came out on a real label (Bronzerat) Steve would not include this song. Therefore it was removed. The song is included with the first two versions of the *Cheap* album (on both the Dead Skunk releases).

So, we can see that within a few months of playing with the Level Devils, Steve had already written most of the songs that weren't released professionally until Bronzerat pressed the album in 2007. (There's A Dead Skunk may have been registered officially by Steve in 2004, the official release date for *Cheap*.) It must have been clear to the other band members that Steve was a dynamic band leader, highly productive songwriter and brilliant guitarist, but, reading between the lines, there is already ample evidence of personal disputes, for which the explanations are mostly speculative.

As we've seen, Morten Gjerde was (and still is) co-founder and co-owner of Bluestown Records, the local label Steve refused to release his album on. The fact that Gjerde resigned as Steve's manager in November 2002, about the time Steve was releasing the first versions of *Cheap* on There's A Dead Skunk Records, suggests that their disagreement was related to this decision. It's easy to understand both sides of the argument: Gjerde must have felt that he was owed a return on his generosity, having put Steve up, introduced him to a band and helped him get his studio off the ground; Steve, who's stubbornly independent at the best of times, probably resented having his artistic freedom curtailed in this way, and perhaps felt that, as a former collaborator with the likes of the Beach Boys, he could do better.

Nor was that the only personality dispute. The identity of this harmonica player, whose contribution to 'Walkin' with the Devil' caused it to be withdrawn from the Bronzerat release, remains a mystery, as does the precise nature of his dispute with Steve. Alongside his ability to create a dazzlingly original sound and reinvent himself musically in the most extraordinary way, Steve also has a knack for personality clashes.

Musically, what stands out from Gjerde's account is Steve's use of the term 'lo-fi blues' to describe his style. We may recall, of course, that 'lo-fi' music was popular on the Olympia scene with figures such as Calvin Johnson. It's obviously applicable to Steve's sound, and matches his whole approach to music, though it's likely he first heard the term in Olympia.

The strangest revelation concerns the label on which the first version of *Cheap* was released. There's a (perhaps inevitable) sense of bitterness, knowing Steve rejected Gjerde's own label, but it does seem weird, when a professional – if rather provincial – record company was offering him a deal. What's even stranger is that Steve should choose to base the label in Clarksdale, Mississippi, somewhere he almost certainly didn't spend much time, if he visited at all. We've already seen how many years Steve spent among the Californian TM community, and the grunge experimentalists of the Northwest, and the Deep South just wasn't home. Even Tennessee he found alien because of the 'Christian bullshit thing'.

At this point, we enter the realms of interpretation rather than demonstrable fact. For what it's worth, my interpretation is that the character of Seasick Steve (and the use of the Clarksdale address) was created to assert Steve's own blues credentials in what were presumably mild attempts by the Norwegians to influence his choice of record label, and possibly other musical decisions. It's open to further question how much of this was conscious planning on Steve's part, and how much instinctive stubbornness and self-preservation. The Mississippi record label Steve created at this point was definitely, in 2002, a fabricated one; and in the same way quite a lot of what he has said as Seasick Steve seems to be urban myth. Steve was insistent on marking out his identity as the senior bluesmen on the scene, even if that meant crossing into the realms of fantasy.

In the matter of the blues, Steve was far more experienced than any of the Norwegian players, however technically good they were. He had played with a handful of the best bluesmen of the 1960s and 1970s, and it's likely that he played with a lot more that we don't know about. So it's understandable he wasn't going to be pushed around by Norwegian players who played a Europeanised blues.

And, without wandering too far into the thickets of amateur psychology, we can say that one consistent feature of Steve's character has been an intense self-reliance, a zealous commitment to the ideals of a project, whether that's TM or independent music, and a determination to be defined according to his own agenda. Sometimes this determination has caused him to give misleading information. He did exactly that when he told *The Stranger* that he'd had a studio in Europe (instead of Tennessee), and he did it here, about both his Clarksdale record label and his hobo past. He cannot have ever have expected to have to repeat this information to more than a few thousand music fans – he ended up having a few million of them.

It's consistent with the evident strength of Steve's ambition that for both Dr Steel and Seasick Steve and the Level Devils, he made a demo CD very early on. He clearly wasn't going to be satisfied with playing pub gigs (or their Norwegian equivalent) for years. These were both serious projects for which he had big plans, and those needed demo CDs. With *Cheap* and *Dog House Music*, it was the demo CDs sent to Joe Cushley and others that led to his breakthrough opportunity.

The tension within the Level Devils did not prevent Steve picking up the job of producing the 2002 compilation album *Christmas in Blue Town*, a communal effort among local musicians that Steve recorded and produced, and that was released in November 2002 on Bluestown Records. It's notable for being (as far as I am aware) the first official release of a Seasick Steve and the Level Devils song. Steve contributed what *Telen* describes as a 'song about the times he in his younger days celebrated Christmas behind bars in US prison' – presumably that was 'Xmas Prison Blues', the same track that he released on *Cheap*. This would represent the first release on an established label, of course – There's A Dead Skunk Records was not that yet.

This is an album strictly for Seasick Steve completists. Only 3,500 were pressed, and I haven't been able to locate a physical copy, although it's still available on iTunes. In the article (published 19 November 2002), Steve assures readers that the album contains 'nothing corny, but good songs that all have their own character'. Suffice to say that 'Xmas Prison Blues' stands out as a serious piece of music-making, even though it's far from clear which Christmas Steve spent behind bars. And it's ironic that his important recording debut as Seasick Steve – more than thirty years since *Shanti* – should be on a light-hearted disc like this.

After the flurry of activity in setting up the studio and starting the new band, 2003 was mostly about consolidation. There was, however, a very successful headline debut for Seasick Steve and the Level Devils on 1 May that year, at the Bellman in Notodden, a well-known local music bar. It's shown briefly in the NRK documentary *Notodden Rock City*, discussed below. As always, *Telen* was on hand to report, in this case in the form of an extensive preview and interview (published on 26 April) outlining Steve's musical philosophy. Steve outlines his musical approach in an intriguing way: '"People can expect the unexpected. We play raw and rough blues where stories are central. Ninety-nine per cent of the lyrics are even experienced things from my own life," says Steve.' He has never been so specific about the autobiographical content of his lyrics before or since. It's as if the truthfulness of the stories is on his mind. Even at this early stage in his career as Seasick Steve, he gives a detailed account of the central story he tells, even though we know that the hobo part of it is almost certainly not true:

> Steve's dream came true just before he turned 14 years old. When he was thrown out of his house and took on several years of life on the road. Often he hitchhiked around or jumped on the freight train, and it was in the wagons he first got experience of life stories told through the blues.

There is much more in this vein. Also noteworthy is that even at this stage, before, frankly, he was in a position to worry about his popularity, he is interested in the issue of young people being put off the blues, something he has clearly thought about in depth. It's almost a musical manifesto:

> My battle aim is to play for most young people who think they do not like blues, and play the blues so they do not know what they hear. Thus I have successfully managed to 'trick' many young people to listen to the blues. I do not demand that they will like it, but they should at least understand that music started before 1990. That even today's music has roots that go back to Charlie Patton and Willie Brown. People who like more punky blues music, like The White Stripes and The Black Keys, will

probably like what we play. Even I have trouble
playing smooth and polished blues. All the music
I grew up with was unsophisticated and unfancy.

As we've seen in earlier chapters, at this stage in his career
Steve is much less guarded about his past, and talks openly
and proudly about his years of playing music professionally:
'Steve spent more and more time around San Francisco,
and in the second half of the Sixties, he played with legends
like . . .' at which point he reels off the names we're already
familiar with.

Great musical debuts are often mundane affairs, but this
one was important because so much of what Steve said
and did was crucial in establishing the persona of 'Seasick
Steve'. And that has remained the same whether he was
playing to fifty people in the Bellman, Notodden, or fifty
thousand at Glastonbury.

The debut gig was reviewed not by *Telen*'s regular music
writer (and occasional musician) Knut H Slettemo, but by
a higher-profile local musician, Trond Ytterbø, who gave it
an absolute rave on 3 May 2003:

Expectations were sky-high, but when Steve Wold
started his raw punky blues, home victory was
secured. What energy and output! Sitting on a
chair with his 1960s Fender Jaguar guitar on a stage
decorated with worn clothes from a tough homeless
life – and floor lamps – such as we had at home in
the Sixties, we became drawn on a unique journey.
Three hours later the band went off stage. Along

with Kai Kristoffersen on drums and J-O Husmo on
bass Seasick Steve & Level Devils have gone down
in history as one of Notodden Blue Club's best
concerts. Thank you and thank you.

It's intriguing that Ytterbø should mention Steve's
thoroughly theatrical addition of 'worn clothes from
a tough homeless life' to the stage. This is something
Steve did for many years afterwards, where there was
time and space to do so. It's a dramatic addition he used
to great effect at his Barbican gigs in January 2009, for
example, but it's fascinating he should have started so
early, at his first full debut. It shows how carefully he
was planning this career. It could also be said to show a
degree of nervousness about the literal truth of his subject
matter: often the most truthful singer-songwriters are the
most stripped back in performance. To create a realistic,
theatrical set for a gig might imply that the artifice of
the material needs help to convince the audience of its
authenticity – or that Steve feels it does.

It's also worth noting that there's no mention at this
stage of any unusual instruments. All available accounts
suggest that Steve started using the Three-String Trance
Wonder and his other trademark adaptations when he was
at home, recuperating after his heart attack and working on
Dog House Music. The hubcap guitars, like the diddley bow
and the three-string, are theatrical props, not something
that evolved from his earlier musical career. Sevrin told
me, 'His three-string guitar is a new thing to suit his hobo-
based performances . . .'

The mood of *Telen*'s coverage changes abruptly on 2 September 2003, however, with the first official news of problems at Juke Joint Studio. Having been owned (with some municipal assistance) and managed entirely by Steve, it seems that a lack of income was causing difficulties two years into the studio's Notodden residency. A formal company board, headed by a local businessman (one Thorbjørn Vassbotn, CEO of Notodden Energy), was put together, and extra investors contributed towards the new company's capital. This opening section of the report not only explains the details of the new agreement but shows how the studio fitted into the town's long-term musical planning:

> Several public and private bodies have now invested money in the legendary Juke Joint Studio in Notodden. Yesterday a limited company was incorporated and thus has secured the studio's future in Notodden.
>
> For it is clear that the owner, American Steve Wold, would have closed the studio and sold it unless he had received financial help from other forces in the city. Fortunately there are many who have seen the value of retaining the unique studio, not least as an important building block in the effort to make Notodden Europe's blue capital with a future Book and Blues House.
>
> It is the foundation of Europe Blues Centre (EBS) which has been running preparatory work leading up to yesterday's foundation meeting, and Jan Erik

Søhoel from EBS [is] very pleased that we now have reached the finish:

'This is a very important addition for blues music in Notodden, and in many ways a milestone in efforts to put Notodden on the European musical map. Now we have secured further presence for the studio, put together a holding company and a board all have faith that we will be able to drive this studio as a good business. We will start promptly seeking new artists who will come to Notodden to record their discs so that we fill up the free studio time, and I will also try to ensure that we can eventually draw artists from countries other than Norway,' says Søhoel.

The article was illustrated with a tense-looking photo of the new board, Steve including, standing in a circle, seething passive aggression. Today, the Book and Blues House ('Bok & Blushuset' in Norwegian) is a state-of-the-art, multipurpose cultural centre, in which the Juke Joint Studio is situated next to a cinema, library, café, college, blues club facilities and 'Blueseum' (Europe's only blues museum, apparently, telling the blues story 'from cotton to Notodden'), and is one of the town's most exciting facilities. Steve's studio is both an active studio and part of the museum. In all probability, given the nature of the local scene, the studio works best in this way, in a kind of public–private partnership.

Although the studio was saved, the situation for Steve personally does not seem to have improved. The

September 2003 deal would have diluted his shareholding, and it dwindled further over the next couple of years, until he finally sold his remaining shares for a pittance in 2005. Espen Fjelle has drawn my attention to an advertisement that Steve placed in *Telen* on 4 August 2005, shortly before that year's Blues Festival, which officially announced his final shares for sale. The translated text runs:

> 400 shares in Juke Joint Studio Ltd, with a total value in 2004 of 443.744 NOK, FOR SALE to the highest bidder over 25.000 NOK. Also interested in swapping with veteran car/motorcycle or vintage guitar. Send your offer to: steve@jukejointstudio.com

The fall in the value of Steve's investment is eye-watering. Though he talks about it wistfully now, after his lucrative breakthrough, at the time it must have been devastating news. The sum Steve was looking for, 25 000 NOK, is about £2,000 at the current exchange rate. When Steve opened the studio in 2001 his share (of 73 per cent of the studio) was valued at 1.9 million NOK, and, as we saw, he could, it's claimed, have sold it for 1.7 million NOK before he left Olympia. In addition, in 2001 Steve owned 73 per cent of the studio; by 2005 the figure was only 31.8 per cent, Fjelle reports. Since 2005 ownership, 67 per cent of which belongs to Fjelle, who is currently employed in the Blues Senter, has remained largely unchanged.

Fjelle reports that the shares were bought by Norwegian harmonica player Arle Hjelmeland, founder of the garage-soul band Good Time Charlie; it's not known if he paid in cash or traded in a car or motorcycle. I have wondered whether Hjelmeland was the harmonica player on *Cheap*, whose dispute with Steve led to the withdrawal of the track 'Walkin' with the Devil', and whose purchase of the shares at this knockdown price may therefore have had a loaded intent. No one has been able to enlighten me, however.

It was a sad end, therefore, for Steve's ownership of the equipment he had so lovingly collected over so many years, which has a modestly distinguished history in both Olympia and Notodden. It is, at least, still in use, unlike so much analogue studio equipment that was eventually simply thrown out. Steve's humour shines through to the end. At least if he was losing his last share in the studio, he could have gained another one of his vintage pleasures – a car, motorbike or guitar, perhaps.

After the formation of the studio company in September 2003, Steve disappears from the pages of *Telen* completely, only to reappear after his *Hootenanny* appearance in early 2007. He was still involved in the management of the studio until his heart attack in 2004, but there's an almost palpable sense of disappointment locally that someone in whom they had such high hopes had fallen short in some way, and – having reported his every move hitherto – *Telen* falls completely silent.

Before we leave the subject of Steve's studio, it's worth turning our attention to two short films that show it in action. As well as blues, there is a fairly active metal scene in the Notodden area. On 28 January 2004, the Norwegian national broadcaster NRK showed a short documentary, entitled *Notodden Rock City – Black Metal Tapes* (available on

YouTube). Acknowledging that the town is mainly known for its blues festival, it goes on to point out that there's a thriving (but smaller) black-metal scene too, and includes an interview with Vegard 'Ihsahn' Tveitan of influential black-metal band Emperor. It also features a discussion with Steve (who speaks English, subtitled into Norwegian), and shows him listening intently to the band's recording. It confirms (as well as a ten-second clip can) what a sensitive and dedicated sound engineer he was, something everyone who's recorded with him agrees on. Aside from his appearance in the Shanti video from more than twenty years earlier, this is the only video footage I am aware of from the period before Steve became famous.

It shows the Juke Joint Studio as Steve set it up, rather less shiny and retro-chic than it appears in the Rival Sons video mentioned below. Yet, as Steve points out in the film, it's there not because it looks cool when polished, and shot in the right light (although it undoubtedly does) but because it sounds good. Steve also tells a story of hearing from musicians in Olympia that Notodden was an important centre of the black-metal scene, something he knew nothing about at the time. He was advised to look it up, and claims to be smitten. It's notable that he was recording such a very different style of music from the blues only two years after setting up in Notodden. His focus on arrival was very much on embedding himself in the blues community, as we've seen. While, on the one hand, it may simply be an interest in finding out about an intriguing and in some ways exotic musical scene he's been recommended, and also to enjoy a breadth of styles, as he did in Olympia, it may also be a further sign that he wasn't getting enough business from the blues community to make a living.

It was shot some time late in 2003, after the Juke Joint Company had been set up to stabilise the studio's finances, and it's not impossible (though impossible to prove at present) that words had been had with NRK, in an attempt to publicise the studio business with younger musicians. It was after Steve had recorded *Cheap*, but before the act had taken its final form, and, as such, is valuable not only in showing Steve at work as a sound engineer, but also in showing the fascinating progression in his appearance from hippie to hobo. He's wearing denim dungarees, of a kind the later Seasick Steve might wear, but a white T-shirt, which later Seasick Steve would rarely sport. Steve's accent is less pronounced than it later becomes, and he speaks more quietly, using more formal idioms. Although he may be just as genuine a part of Steve's character as the more softly spoken sound engineer, there's no doubt 'Seasick' Steve is a different personality.

As well as the Norwegian documentary, bands' music videos have been shot in Juke Joint Studios, though the latest of these show the studio in its new location in the Book and Blues Senter, having been buffed up to pristine, museum condition. One of the most beautifully shot examples is for the song 'Long As I Can See the Light', by Long Beach blues rockers Rival Sons, recorded on 31 July 2014 (available on YouTube). It's filmed in black and white, and the gear does look seductively retro. Billed as a collaboration between the band's record label, Earache, the Notodden Blues Festival and the studio itself, it suggests an approach to business – with multi-party contracts, and complex tie-ins involving festival appearances connected to studio time – that perhaps Steve had neither the time, resources or inclination to pursue. Rival Sons performed that same evening in Hovigs Hangar, Notodden, as part of the festival line-up. As we've seen, in Olympia most bookings seemed to arrive by word of mouth, which works fine on a busy scene like Olympia's, but is less effective in a small, remote Scandinavian town.

Presumably, Steve continued to work at the studio until he had his heart attack. The final, ignominious sale of his last shares in 2005 came after the attack, but, after the difficulties of September 2003 and the new management, he must have been under a lot of stress. Steve has said very little about the event itself, and at the time of writing there is no one who can shine a light on the subject. Suffice it to say that at some point early in 2004, he had a heart attack in the night. With Steve's paramedic training, and his wife's quick thinking, the urgency of his situation was recognised and he was taken to hospital in an ambulance. Thereafter, he was able to spend months recuperating at home, thanks to Norway's generous social security.

There is a detailed account in Steve's January 2009 interview in *The Daily Mail*, in which he pays tribute to Elisabeth's quick reactions – although the accuracy of some of this version, which states that Steve was living in Oslo (not Notodden) at the time, is suspect.

'Luckily, we were only ten minutes from the hospital. If we'd been another 15 minutes away, I don't think I'd have pulled through.

'Elizabeth [*sic*] was in bed with me and she knew straight away what was going on. She called the ambulance and they fixed me up. It was all pretty horrible.'

It was as he was recovering – 'a long and painful process' – that Steve turned, once again, to music.

Steve's son Sevrin described the event as 'his little heart attack'. How much weight we should attach to the 'little' is debatable. But unless Sevrin has made up his whole story about Steve's final visit – and in every other respect he has been absolutely reliable – Steve seems within a few weeks to have been able to live a relatively normal life again, and must have returned to the American Northwest in 2004 to see Sevrin and his family, and presumably old friends from Olympia. He also visited London late that year.

It's now well known that Steve used his recuperation to write and record the songs on *Dog House Music*. There are a few important stages to record before he started doing that, however. Before he began playing solo he seems to have got busy sending out the CDs of *Cheap* he'd recorded in 2002, in order to secure some overseas gigs and radio airtime. The official history of There's A Dead Skunk Records is also closely guarded, but it's possible, if not likely, that at some point in 2004 Steve registered the company officially, so that he could release *Cheap* formally on that label. The official release date is always given as 2004, even though, as we know, it was recorded in 2002, and Steve had unofficial copies ready for distribution then. It wasn't rereleased by Bronzerat Records until early 2007. So the 2004 release date, unless simply an error, must reflect the fact that this is when There's A Dead Skunk Records became a real record company.

Steve must have sent DJs and promoters a CD, because at that time he had no other credentials, bar a couple of reviews (in Norwegian, pre-Google Translate) in *Telen*. His first UK gig was reportedly at the 12 Bar Club in Denmark Street, Soho, in late 2004. *NME* reported in May 2013, in a profile of the bar (which has sadly since closed): 'Seasick Steve played his first (and very impromptu) UK show here in 2004, to a handful of people.' Other, more formal gigs followed at the same venue, and he began to make a name for himself as a solo performer on the blues scene in London in 2005 and 2006.

But the gig that reportedly turned him into a confident solo performer was in Belfast. *The Belfast Telegraph* reported the story in September 2010, which is part crucial biography, and part, as is typical with Steve, charming anecdote:

> The American blues singer made his first-ever headlining appearance as a solo artist at the John Hewitt pub back in 2005 as part of the Coors Light Open House Festival.
>
> Since that gig his career has taken off, and he has performed at various festivals around the world as well as receiving the 2007 MOJO award for Best Breakthrough Act.
>
> But the musician, who worked behind the scenes in production before getting his break out front, hasn't forgotten his roots and will be back headlining the Open House Festival again this month.

To commemorate that historical gig in Belfast five years ago, Seasick Steve will be presented with a silver plaque that will be unveiled at the John Hewitt pub during the festival.

Speaking ahead of his Belfast show Seasick Steve, whose real name is Steven Wold, said the 2005 gig was a turning point.

'It's probably the reason I'm playing music,' he said.

'If I hadn't done that gig at the Open House Festival in Belfast, I don't think I'd be playing music now.'

His debut gig as a solo artist was on October 2 and the date clashed with a photographic exhibition called Hobo, which was also taking place at the John Hewitt pub.

The festival organisers had problems trying to hang the pictures up and, as a result, the concertgoers were forced to wait an extra hour outside the pub.

A spokeswoman for Open House said: 'Instead of just leaving them out there, Seasick Steve went outside into the street and busked for them and the crowd got bigger. When the doors opened, everyone was let in for free and the place was packed.'

What Steve hasn't explained here is why this was a solo gig, and didn't include the Level Devils. When he travelled to London in 2004, and performed at the 12 Bar Club, he wasn't initially expecting to perform, and in the first instance there is a question of practicality: these were small gigs abroad with little or no money, and it was just easier for Steve to do them alone rather than pay for the Level Devils too. Although there may, as we'll see, be more to it. This transition has been glossed over in public, but there are some hints in an interview Steve gave to *musicOMH* in August 2008. He tells interviewer Michael Hubbard:

'When I started feeling a little better I tried to play a bit after, but I didn't feel too good. I'd set up a few shows over here, I was gonna come and play in Belfast. But I had to cancel it.' And that could have been the end of it all, had some tenacious promoters in Northern Ireland decided to let up. 'Those people kept calling me up, as they'd kinda made a big deal of it. They said why don't you come over by yourself and we'll take care of you?'

It sounds as though Steve had originally booked the gig to include the Level Devils, but, after he cancelled, the promoters asked him over 'by yourself'. There is, however, some uncertainty about the background to this story. Steve had, as we've seen, travelled to see his son in Olympia, and to play in Soho, nearly a year earlier. If he was well enough to make those trips, it's a little mysterious he should not feel able to make the short trip to Belfast. Is this to cover up another disagreement? Had Steve decided to cut himself loose from his Norwegian ties completely, even from bassist Jo Husmo, with whom Steve jammed back in September 2001, at what must be considered the official inauguration of Seasick Steve? They do seem to have been cut adrift rather brutally, although Steve is obviously still on good terms with Swedish drummer Papa Dan. We will probably never know.

In any case, the official explanation for Steve's decision to perform solo is the ecstatic reception he got at his Belfast gig, as he explained to *musicOMH*:

> I went over there and played by myself and everybody was going crazy. When I got back and told her [his wife, Elisabeth] she was like, 'Why don't you just sit in the kitchen there with an old four track tape recorder and make some songs? Not like you do with a band, but just like you do when you're sitting at home.' So that's what I did.'

This, then, is the origin of *Dog House Music*. It's also the origin of his beat-up three-string guitar. This is how Steve explained it to *The Independent* in September 2008:

> It was she [Elisabeth], again, who foresaw the significance of the Trance Wonder. 'That guitar is so bad,' he says with a chuckle. 'It's some Japanese guitar from the Sixties. I still string it the way it was when I got it. Not one string is in the right slot. I wasn't going to play it, but a friend in Norway who repairs guitars asked me to show it to him. My wife was in the kitchen doing the dishes and she saw me out on the front lawn with that guy. He said, "You can't play that," and I said, "Yes, I can," and I just started playing some riff on it. And

he laughed and drove away. I brought the guitar inside and my wife goes, "That guitar's gonna make you famous."'

There's a good argument that, of all Steve's albums, *Dog House Music* represents the purest form of the blues. While *Cheap* was recorded in 2002 when Steve still seemed confident about the studio's future, and all of his subsequent albums, from 2008's *I Started Out With Nothin* . . . onwards, were made when he was prosperous and successful, in *Dog House Music*, Steve is really feeling the blues. It's more raw, bleak, isolated and depressing than any of his others, and the sound of the recording suits him – and the blues – better.

We've seen that throughout his career, Steve has shown a knack for emphasising the picturesque elements of his career, while consistently downplaying the sheer force of his ambition. Busking in Belfast makes for a lovely story, but the likelihood is that as soon as Steve had made contact with the people on the London blues scene who would lead him to his breakthrough – at least a year before the Belfast gig – the Level Devils became irrelevant. He had a band, Dr Steel, lined up for album release and international tour in 2000; by September 2001 they were forgotten, and Seasick Steve was born. Once he had a new stage in London, the Level Devils went the same way.

In order to get even an impromptu gig at the 12 Bar Club, Steve would have needed an introduction, and it's most likely that the Resonance FM DJ Joe Cushley – who has the most sensitive antennae for promising newcomers on the London blues scene – recommended him to DJ Andy Lowe of the 12 Bar Club. A BBC Berkshire preview, still available online, of Steve's gig in Newbury in March 2007 – only a couple of months after his breakthrough – gives us a good idea of the holy trinity of Steve's supporters in the London media:

> Charlie Gillett, legendary radio DJ and author of what has become the bible on black music in America, *Sound Of The City*, says Seasick Steve has brought him back to the blues and is the 'first blues artist in 20 years to really move him'.
>
> Mark Ellen, *The Old Grey Whistle Test* presenter, and past editor of *MOJO* and *Q* and now *Word* magazine, has featured Steve several times and has also been to every show Steve has done in London.
>
> Joe Cushley, past writer for *MOJO* and now writing for London's *What's On* magazine and London FM Resonance radio DJ has stated simply that 'Seasick Steve is probably the greatest live bluesman on the planet' and regularly plays Seasick's music on his shows.

This is the influential trio who got Steve on *Hootenanny*. Gillett died in 2010. Cushley is now a close friend of Steve's, and as such was not willing to contribute to my research. Gillett played Steve on his BBC Radio show *World on 3* occasionally, even before his breakthrough. Andy Zammit, owner of Bronzerat Records, which released *Dog House Music* in December 2006, and licensed *Cheap* from

Steve's own label to release in April 2007, didn't get to know Steve until 2006.

I am assuming, then, that Steve sent Joe Cushley a homemade copy of *Cheap* in 2004. Cushley immediately recognised the talent and provided regular encouragement and support, inviting Steve to London for gigs at the 12 Bar Club from late 2004 onwards. These were all attended by Mark Ellen, sometimes by Charlie Gillett too. Although the parties involved have not confirmed it with me directly, it's the only way the events we know took place could have happened. We know that Steve referred to Cushley as a friend as early as 2006, when Cushley rang Steve to see how he was getting on with *Dog House Music*. When Steve's second album was finished, Cushley recommended it to Andy Zammit at Bronzerat, who then became involved in the increasingly hectic *Hootenanny* chase, with the assistance of Steve's three other media supporters, in December that year. Zammit was working at that time as a tour manager, and as such drove bands to the BBC studios, and was on the spot most regularly to hand over demo CDs. It was a frantic team effort.

Steve and his family retain close links to Norway, and Steve's sons with Elisabeth still live there at least some of the time, but musically he seems to have severed all connections. Steve played the Notodden Blues Festival with the Level Devils in 2002 and 2003, but that second festival appearance is the last recorded performance in the town. There remains some mystery as to how Steve came to bring over a modestly successful studio business with much valuable equipment and lose much of his money in less than five years. Having heard only one side of the story, it's dangerous to draw definite conclusions. It is clear, however, that Notodden deserves more recognition as the musical birthplace of Seasick Steve than it usually gets. It was here that he was put up and introduced to his first band. Here, he wrote most of the early songs, and had both his live and recording debut. He received his first rave review for his raw punk blues in Notodden, and established the hobo aesthetic there that has proven such a hit with fans.

From 2004 onwards, London was the centre of Steve's career, and he seems to have cultivated his contacts there much more assiduously than he lets on. However, not even Steve could have predicted the extraordinary consequences when Andy Zammit's demo CD got through to the *Hootenanny* producers, and – with the support of Joe Cushley, Charlie Gillett and Mark Ellen – the show's final spot was given to this completely unknown American with some tall tales about trains.

CHAPTER 9

London and the world

The effect of Steve's *Hootenanny* performance was immediately apparent on his own website, but his media profile and record sales took longer to get going. He won forty per cent of the poll for the night's best performer on the *Hootenanny* website, far ahead of everyone else, including Paul Weller, Amy Winehouse, Lily Allen and the Kooks, but it took a busy summer of festival appearances, and the trickle-down of media reports and word of mouth for him to become a major star, as he did in 2008. *I Started Out With Nothin And I Still Got Most of It Left*, released in September that year, is the only one of his albums to be certified platinum. *Dog House Music* reached only No. 36 in the UK charts, whereas five of the six subsequent albums all made the top ten, and even *Hubcap Music* – the only one of the five not to do so – was still certified Gold.

There's a sense from some of the coverage that critics

were expecting Steve to fade away, back to his boxcar, and neither *Dog House Music* nor *Cheap* received many high-profile reviews. One critic who seems determined to make a point about *Cheap* is AllMusic's Richie Unterberger. This is the same music writer who contributed the album notes for the rerelease of *Shanti*, so he clearly knew who Steve was and where he came from. You don't need to be hypersensitive to hear the sarcasm in Unterberger's description of 'the mysterious Seasick Steve'.

Moreover, Unterberger is underwhelmed by both the novelty and musical quality of Steve's album, arguing that *Cheap* 'would have been more ear-catching had it come out ten years or so earlier, before other people did similar stuff (and sometimes did it better)'. While other critics have noted Steve's samey sounds after three or four albums, Unterberger is unusual in regarding Seasick Steve as a derivative project from the start. This is a surprisingly damning judgement. Though few other critics reviewed *Cheap*, waiting for *Dog House Music* or even *I Started Out With Nothin*, Unterberger's laconic tone is completely out of keeping with the generally breathless enthusiasm of the British media. This is partly, of course, because Unterberger knew the scene Steve was drawing on stylistically much better than most British critics. Is there also resentment about Steve's 'mysterious' persona here? Hard to say. Unterberger does refer to 'the hard-living hobo life', rather than 'Steve's hobo life'.

The songs are basic, repetitive, and slightly grungy, Steve singing in a lived-in, scratchy, at times mumbly voice that might slightly remind you of Tom Waits and Dr John at times, though it's not really that close to either of them. The program's interrupted by a couple of rambling spoken monologues about the hard-living hobo life, and the songs tend to ramble on without saying much as well. The result is a record that's at once idiosyncratically down-home and kind of forgettable . . .

One day, when the cat is finally out of the bag, it would be fascinating to hear what the American musical press thinks about Steve's rise. I have no doubt his identity is an open secret in parts of the American musical community. Some, such as the Olympia posse, are probably friends, but, given Steve's apparent propensity for making enemies, there may well be a few more who have been itching to bust him.

As for Unterberger's comments about the music, it would be useful to hear which 'oldsters and youngsters' he thinks have been recording music better than Steve's. Even a master such as R L Burnside, whom Steve knew a little, and who was recording at the times Unterberger specifies, manages to sound more formulaic to the traditions of the blues than Steve. The sound palette is similar, but Steve usually breaks some rules, and does something unexpected. *Cheap* is certainly not Steve's best work, but there's still a freshness and spontaneity about his musical structures, his lyrics and his sound, which is why he appeals so readily outside a traditional blues audience while sounding, at first anyway, very similar.

SEASICK STEVE

Among the early reviews of Seasick Steve's work, Rick Webb is on the money in his January 2007 bluesinlondon. com review of *Dog House Music*, pointing out that 'he plays music that is squarely rooted in the heart of "blues", yet he does it absolutely on his own terms and without pandering to the cliché and conservatism that has come to dominate the genre', and that there is 'an extraordinary repertoire of songs'. The fact that Steve writes about a far wider range of topics than a traditional bluesman is often overlooked. 'For all his primitive vibe Steve's nowhere near as naïve as he makes out and this a sophisticated record made by a man who knows exactly what he's doing. The result is a cohesive album . . .' Spontaneity, variety, authenticity (of emotion, if not of biographic fact) and raw acoustic heft are what makes Steve's act great.

His festival tour of summer 2007 was famously active, with – reportedly – more performances than any other musician, including four at Glastonbury, with Reading, Leeds, Green Man, Latitude and Bestival among his crowded itinerary. Steve is perfectly adapted to the British festival scene: humorous, patient, full of stories, completely unflappable, waterproof and able to charm anyone, he has been a hit from the start. His habit of inviting a woman from the audience to sing 'Walkin Man' to always seems to endear him to the crowd, however many times he does it. With his age and appearance, he can get away with being flirtatious, even when wearing what *NME* described (in July 2009) as 'a wifebeater-style vest'.

Steve's instinctive charm and storytelling ability enable him to pace evening-long comfortably. The theatre of his live shows also helps. He's stopped now bringing a laundry's worth of old clothes to hang about the set, as he did on his Notodden debut, and in the Barbican in 2009, but there are still the hubcaps, washboards, diddley bows and the rest to amuse and distract. And the chemistry with drummer Dan Magnusson (Papa-Dan), who's been together with Steve on and off for more than a decade, means they can stretch the pieces any old way and make it different each time, and still work. These are the key features of his live gigs and festival sets, which sell out year after year.

It became obvious in the eighteen months following his breakthrough that Steve would be an enduring presence. This was partly to do with the Mojo award he won on 18 June 2007, soon after his breakout. He won for Best Breakthrough Act, beating some artists now at least as well known as he is, such as Joanna Newsom. Hearing Mojo's shortlist compilation film that sets Steve's grainy, weather-beaten rasp alongside Newsom's artful caterwauling is a surreal experience.

At the ceremony, Steve appeared to be ready to shuffle off stage without saying anything. His Mojo acceptance speech (it's on YouTube) was short and to the point: 'I've been breaking through for forty-five years. I've got some more breaking to do.' It described his musical career more succinctly than the tales of blue-collar jobs that he's told ever since.

Steve has subsequently been nominated for other awards: Mojo Best Live Act in 2008 and 2011, and a Brit Award nomination for International Solo Male Artist in 2009. But, as a live act, he's outperformed his prize haul significantly:

there are many musicians with more gongs than Steve who couldn't hope to sell out venues over nearly a decade with the frequency he has. *The Independent* declared that Steve was 'toast of the festival circuit for the second summer in a row' back in September 2008, and he's maintained that status ever since. Whether it's based on real experience or (as we've seen is more likely) imaginative recreation, this popularity is testament to the emotional authenticity of his act, and his ability to be seemingly free of showbiz pizzazz and artifice.

The Mojo award and Steve's incredible summer of festival gigs consolidated his profile sufficiently for the mainstream media to take notice. Starting with *The Telegraph* in September 2007, *The Guardian* and *Independent* following suit in August and September 2008 respectively, and *The Daily Mail* tagging along in January 2009, the press gave Steve the kind of feature-length exposure reserved for *bona fide* stars. We've already looked at the content of most of these; there's a lot of human interest and fascinating detail despite the overemphasis on his hobo life, which many of the writers seem to suspect is overegged but can't help themselves repeating. The less said about BBC Four's short documentary, *Bringing It Back Home*, the better. It's debatable whether Steve has a home at all, and even less so his particular music, which is many things as well as blues; but, if you were to nominate a place, it would have to be San Francisco, not Mississippi.

After Steve's extraordinary summer of 2007, record companies also decided to get a piece of the action, and Warner Music offered him a deal he couldn't refuse. So this stalwart of the independent music scene went on to record for a major label – ironically, the one he was signed to with Shanti back in 1971.

We've already read the endearing story Steve tells about the way he persuaded his wife to give up her exhausting job in an old people's home and stay with him recording *I Started With Nothin* at Leeder's Farm Studio in south Norfolk. It's not a pleasant duty to be forever pouring cold water on Steve's charming stories, but since, by this point, *Cheap* and *Dog House Music* had been selling well, and he'd played dozens of big summer festivals, was his wife really still doing a backbreaking job in an old people's home? Or is this another distraction from the real issue of his major-label contract?

Remember the Tremens' remark about Steve – that his attitude towards fame was 'God forgive the soul who wants to be a rock star'? At some point quite soon after his breakthrough, he seems to have decided that – after his studio failed, and left him with nothing to fall back on other than performance – he would make the best of it, even though he clearly feels uncomfortable letting people glimpse his true self. With a hobo alter ego to deflect much of the celebrity intrusion, perhaps he felt safe.

So he embraced a major label, Warner Bros. After two albums with them, he has changed again with each release, to Play It Again Sam, then Fiction Records, then Caroline International – each time for more money, presumably. Unfortunately, there is no available background information to shed any light on the process. Andy Zammit of Bronzerat Records, who had released Steve's first two albums, and released the vinyl (though not the CD) of *I Started Out With Nothin . . .*, had nothing further to add.

Steve and Elisabeth appear to have stayed on in south Norfolk for a year or two after the recording, and then moved to Cornwall, for greater seclusion and better surfing, with a flat in Norway for visiting family. From a biographical point of view, however, despite the high-profile gigs, his life is much less interesting than it used to be.

Although there's a general consensus that *I Started Out With Nothin . . .* and *Man From Another Time* are his best major albums, there's an even clearer consensus on the best way forward for Steve. Critics are agreed that more of the same is not an attractive option. As Alex Petridis noted in his *Guardian* review (September 2008) of *I Started Out With Nothin . . .*, 'you might ask precisely how many albums of hobo-themed blues rock a man needs'. Petridis finds the album's title track depressingly tame: 'with its smooth guitars and surfeit of female vocals, it sounds like something designed with local radio . . . in mind: a depressingly neutered take on Wold's sound'. But, when Steve moves on to new musical territory, he still has the power to shock and amaze, as he does with the final track, 'My Youth'. It's a wistful, jangling, guitar-sliding reverie, as much country as blues; as Petridis says, it's 'a desolate meditation on ageing, it's the best thing here, and there's not a hint of the dusty tracks [of Steve's hobo songs] about it'.

As the years passed critics became less tolerant of songs that don't step off the well-worn path. Concluding that the music works 'best when Steve tries some experimentation',

Nathan Stevens, reviewing *Sonic Soul Surfer* in *Popmatters*, declares the album to be 'one of the most frustrating albums of 2015 so far'. Stevens applauds three songs – 'In Peaceful Dreams', 'Right On Time' and 'Heart Full Of Scars' – all of which move the sound on from traditional hobo-blues territory. 'Right on Time' has Steve revealing a tender falsetto that's wounded yet potent, while the last is, in Stevens's words, 'quietly stunning'. His conclusion, however, is on the whole less positive: 'Seasick Steve wheezes and growls his way through *Sonic Soul Surfer*, showing a few new cards up his sleeve, but mostly sticking to a tired and true blues crawl.' Perhaps it would be best for Steve's music, as well as his biography, to move on to completely new musical territory.

Aside from Unterberger's early critique, Steve has generally avoided a critical pasting for good reasons, although, as critics became more familiar with his approach, one or two couldn't resist venting their frustration when his approach touched on self-parody – always a danger with a retro act. A piece like Jeremy Allen's review of *Hubcap Music* in *NME* (April 2013) is best seen as a reminder to keep his focus sharp, and avoid lazy repetition at all costs. Allen is decidedly unimpressed by Steve's improvised hubcap guitar, musing that Steve 'might have made a trip to Denmark Street to get himself a proper guitar by now', and judging the 'purring pickup truck at the outset and conclusion' to be merely a ploy to 'remind us just how down-at-heel and blue-collar he really is'. The props don't matter at all, however, when the music is so mediocre, argues Allen: 'tracks such as 'Down on the Farm' deliver

SEASICK STEVE

the kind of boogie-woogie twattery Shania Twain would have her writing team skinned for.'

As Steve's fame reached its peak, he was invited to play some high-profile venues that he made much of at the time. In October 2008, he sold out the Royal Albert Hall, delighting both fans and critics with what most agreed were triumphantly entertaining performances. As Ian Gittins observed in his *Guardian* review: 'After tonight's hugely entertaining, at times staggering show, it is hard to imagine that any of the veteran bluesman's devotees went home remotely disappointed.' Again, one lucky lady was serenaded for 'Walkin Man', and he told some of his usual stories. According to Gittins, Steve repeatedly confessed his shock at being allowed to play the Royal Albert Hall. However, Steve's incredulity is a little harder to take at face value when we bear in mind this is someone whose band was, some forty years earlier, sharing the bill with Joan Baez at the Hollywood Bowl, and Ali Akbar Khan at the San Francisco Palace of Fine Arts.

Musically, Steve's new fame gave him access to celebrity collaborators. It must have been fun for him, though it didn't necessarily improve the music. On *I Started Out With Nothin . . .* there's Nick Cave (with Grinderman), who, according to Alex Petridis, 'turns in a brilliantly restrained performance on "Just Like a King", which is alternately brooding, lascivious and hilarious: "I'm a prizefighter baby, when I step inside your ring."' This album also features K T Tunstall on guitar and Ruby Turner as lyricist, though, as we shall see in the case of other albums that have too much instrumentation – *Hubcap Music*, mainly – it can handicap the most distinctive features of Steve's performance in an unfortunate way.

Bassist John Paul Jones of Led Zeppelin joined in for the 2011 album *You Can't Teach An Old Dog New Tricks*, and also performed with Steve three times at festival gigs that summer: Isle of Wight in June, Latitude in July and Reading in August. Although it must have been a lot of fun for all concerned, Jones doesn't seem to have made much difference, musically. The most positive review of the album came from the BBC's Chris Lo:

> The album stretches to new band members too, with erstwhile Led Zep bassist John Paul Jones and drummer Dan Magnusson joining Wold on several tracks to provide a punchy rhythm section he has hitherto denied himself. It's an effective partnership; the extra power on 'Back in the Doghouse' pushes the Seasick sound ever further into rock'n'roll crossover territory.

By the time we come to *Hubcap Music* (2013), Steve had not just Jones but also Jack White on board. Many critics felt that Steve had rather overdone the extra musical backup, and created something that wasn't true to his own aesthetic, as Hilary Saunders in *Paste Magazine* explains in one of the politer reviews:

> Jack White's influence can be felt on *Hubcap Music*, Steve's second record on Third Man Records, although a number of other impressive guests

including John Paul Jones and Luther Dickinson also contributed. The extra musicianship certainly creates a richer sound, but sometimes feels excessive: 'The Way I Do' evokes like Danger Mouse-era Black Keys, 'Coast is Clear' features gospel-style 'ooh's' and thick keys, and 'Heavy Weight' layers both rhythm and lead guitars over Steve's scat harmonies.

As someone who advocates *Dog House Music* as Steve's most essential performance, I would agree with this criticism, though there's no doubt that White added some fun and dazzle. We must remember that in an earlier life Steve had been playing, on and off, with celebrity musicians of White's stature for decades, so must enjoy their stardust.

For some observers, another media highlight was Steve's appearance on *Top Gear* with Jeremy Clarkson in January 2010. It's significant as an indication of how far Steve's appeal reached out from the specialist musical niche in which he was well concealed only five years earlier. We don't learn a great deal new about Steve. We already knew he liked talking about cars, and he seems a little overawed, perhaps, as he exhibits the same strange, blinking-into-the-stagelight tic he also displayed on *Hootenanny*. But it is an extraordinary testament to his appeal across class, sex and age that a singer of ultimately quite specialist music can cross over in this way. His charm is uncanny.

It would be wonderful to think that Steve will one day tell his own story, and the glorious details of exactly whom he played with throughout the sixties and eighties.

Unfortunately, it's unlikely, if he's hung on this long to his alter ego with the bindle and diddley bow, riding the boxcar. In many ways, the bottomless charm and gregarious exterior is a defence mechanism. He takes control of conversations, steering them away from sensitive topics by distraction, reciting an alternative version of events or simply feigning forgetfulness.

There is much about Seasick Steve that is deeply private. His wife is very rarely seen at public events, and his children appear only when they are – like Paul Martin – involved in his performances. He has gone out of his way, too, to divert any attention to his past (and present?) interest in Transcendental Meditation, even though that interest is commonplace among musicians and hardly a cause for embarrassment. And the full story of his musical career, something that he's pursued with concentrated ambition throughout his life, has generally been kept well hidden – unless he's with people he trusts (the Tremens) or those he thinks aren't likely to pass the news on (the Norwegian blues community). Look at the overreaction to the loss of the Shanti recording contract – 'everything has gone down the shitter'. The other musicians in the band got on with their careers. Steve went away for five years, finding it much harder to rebuild when he returned. He's much more highly strung than his image lets on.

He undoubtedly had some very lonely times when he was very young – despite landing on his feet in Haight-Ashbury at pivotal moment in popular culture – including a difficult start to his musical career, without any of the emotional or material support many young musicians get from family. Because of that isolation and fragility, he appears to feel highly sensitive about topics that others cheerfully discuss openly, and so has wrapped himself in amnesiac hobo cotton wool. When he's in the mood, though, is there a live entertainer to match him? Listening to his wonderful stories on stage, it's easy to forget that there are some much, much better ones waiting untold in his memory – if only he can bring himself to tell them.

Acknowledgements

A ll books are a tapestry of shared contributions. A biography, especially one whose subject is retiring about the facts of his own life, is especially so. Some sources have remained silent, but enough have come forward to uncover an extraordinary and unexpected life story.

Firstly, I am grateful to Sevrin Johnson, Steve's eldest son, and leader of the band Peratus, for sharing some of his recollections of growing up with (and without) Steve. Morten Gjerde and Espen Fjelle, important figures on the blues scene of Notodden, Norway, have generously assisted with crucial new information about Steve's time in the area, much of which would have been impossible to find any other way.

Colleagues at *The Arts Desk* have been supportive throughout, but particular thanks go to the inspirational Thomas H Green, who has, in the magnificent series of

SEASICK STEVE

Q&As he has conducted for the site, led by example in the mining of musical character. And it was through his generous intervention that the project came to life in the first place.

Many friends have helped me with both practical and emotional assistance at what has been a complicated time for me to write a book. Their support has been a model of friendship.

Discography

Albums

Shanti (as Steve Leach), Atlantic, 1971
Cheap (with the Level Devils), There's A Dead Skunk, 2004
/ Bronzerat, 2007*
Doghouse Music, Bronzerat, 2006
I Started Out With Nothin And I Still Got Most Of It Left,
Warner Music UK Ltd, 2008
Man From Another Time, Atlantic, 2009
You Can't Teach An Old Dog New Tricks, Play It Again Sam,
2011
Hubcap Music, Fiction Records, 2013
Live At Third Man Records, Third Man Records, 2013
Sonic Soul Surfer, There's A Dead Skunk Records, 2015

Singles & EPs

It's All Good, Bronzerat, 2007
'Things Go Up' (CDR Promo), Bronzerat, 2007

SEASICK STEVE

'Walkin Man', Rhino Records, 2008
'Happy Man / St Louis Slim' (CDR Promo), Warner Music
UK Ltd, 2008
'Diddly Bo', Rykodisc, 2010
'Write Me A Few Lines', Third Man Records, 2011
'You Can't Teach An Old Dog New Tricks', Play It Again
Sam, 2011
'It's A Long Long Way' (CDR Promo), Play It Again Sam,
2011
'Down on the Farm' (CDR Promo), Universal, 2013
'Coast Is Clear' (CDR Promo), Universal, 2013
'Bring It On', There's A Dead Skunk Records, 2015
'Summertime Boy', There's A Dead Skunk Records, 2015

Compilations
Songs For Elisabeth, Atlantic, 2010
Walkin Man, The Best Of, Rhino Records, 2011

Miscellaneous
'Christmas In Bluestown', Bluestown Records, 2002
(Seasick Steve and the Level Devils play track 5, 'Xmas
Prison Blues')
'Started Out With Nothin' (CDR Promo), Warner Bros
Records, 2008
'Ready For Love' (CDR Promo), Atlantic, 2010
'Roy's Gang' (CDR Promo), There's A Dead Skunk
Records, 2015

*Copies of the album under the There's A Dead Skunk
logo were available from 2004, but the status of the There's
A Dead Skunk company in 2004 is unclear.